Real Estate Investing for First-Timers

The Exposed Secrets on Sourcing Down Payment for First Time Home Buyers

D.Y. Michael

© **Copyright 2021 - All rights reserved.**

The content contained within this book may not be reproduced, duplicated or transmitted without direct written permission from the author or the publisher.

Under no circumstances will any blame or legal responsibility be held against the publisher, or author, for any damages, reparation, or monetary loss due to the information contained within this book, either directly or indirectly.

Legal Notice:

This book is copyright protected. It is only for personal use. You cannot amend, distribute, sell, use, quote or paraphrase any part, or the content within this book, without the consent of the author or publisher.

Disclaimer Notice:

Please note the information contained within this document is for educational and entertainment purposes only. All effort has been executed to present accurate, up to date, reliable, complete information. No warranties of any kind are declared or implied. Readers acknowledge that the author is not engaged in the rendering of legal, financial, medical or professional advice. The content within this book has been derived from various sources. Please consult a licensed professional before attempting any techniques outlined in this book.

By reading this document, the reader agrees that under no circumstances is the author responsible for any losses, direct or indirect, that are incurred as a result of the use of the information contained within this document, including, but not limited to, errors, omissions, or inaccuracies.

Table of Contents

INTRODUCTION 1

CHAPTER 1: CROWDFUNDING YOUR WAY TO HOMEOWNERSHIP 5

    TYPES OF CROWDFUNDING 8
        How to Raise Money.. 12
        Show Appreciation.. 15
        Understand the Costs 16

CHAPTER 2: BUILD A LINE OF CREDIT 17

    SECURED VS. UNSECURED 20
        Types of Credit 23

CHAPTER 3: CONSIDER 100% FINANCING: THE USDA HOME LOAN 27

    HOW TO QUALIFY 30
        The Pros and Cons 34

CHAPTER 4: POOR CREDIT SCORE? NO WORRIES; TAKE AN FHA LOAN 39

    UNDERSTANDING THE FHA 40
        Types of FHA Loans.. 45

CHAPTER 5: ARE YOU A VETERAN? CONSIDER VA LOANS.................... 51

    THE APPLICATION PROCESS 53
        Benefits and Drawbacks 58

CHAPTER 6: SAVE UP!... 65

    AUTOMATE YOUR SAVINGS FOR A DOWN PAYMENT 70
        Seven Smart Investment Strategies 73

CHAPTER 7: HOW ABOUT...DOWNSIZING?...................................... 79

    HOW TO DOWNSIZE BEFORE YOU UPSIZE 80
        The Benefits and Disadvantages....................................... 84

CHAPTER 8: YOU COULD ALSO MAKE MORE MONEY 91

    MAKING EXTRA CASH 92

Passive Income 96
CONCLUSION 103
REFERENCES 107

"To buy a nice home is to buy a better way of life. To choose a better way of life is to work toward well-being, and isn't well-being what's paramount?"

-by Anonymous

Introduction

Nothing feels better than arriving at the comfort of home after a hard day. Until that home has a For Sale sign in the yard, and you know that not one penny of it is going into your pocket. After years of lovingly caring for this house, investing memories, money, sweat, and tears into its upkeep, it's being taken from you. Nothing momentous needed to happen, just a simple letter from your landlord stating that you needed to move since they decided to sell. All the years of investments in upkeep and emotions are gone. What was once a comforting sight now looms before you as a desolate house that is moving on without you.

For centuries, people have yearned for a stable place to live. Somewhere they can raise families, build memories, and have the solid comfort in knowing they have a safe place to return after a day of challenges. However, it can often feel as if only a select chosen can own this dream. Too many people are lifelong renters who risk losing their homes to the whims of their landlords. Too many children are left bewildered that the home they've been raised in is suddenly gone from their lives. Many times, this is simply because people are under the illusion that owning a home is for the wealthy or fortunate. They feel their meager jobs or financial status won't allow them to be homeowners, and over time, they give up hope and settle into the rental rut.

Living in someone else's home where they get all of the benefits is not what the majority of people desire. It's what they settled for. The only time you should be settling is when you have the deed to your own home. There are a multitude of ways people in many different situations can own homes of their own. The problem is, no one ever teaches this in schools. This book will guide you step by step through the variety of options out there. Everyone, with the right education and discipline, is a potential homeowner. And it isn't only the lucky ones who become real homeowners. It's the people who have never given up on the dream of owning something they will have for the rest of their lives. Or an investment that they can profit from, not the landlord.

This is not an easy journey. It can often be overwhelming, but perseverance is key. Owning a home is the pinnacle of aspiration for many, and it can seem unachievable at times. However, you will learn the key points of crowdfunding, how to build credit, facts about different types of loans, such as USDA, FHA, and VA, tips on how to save, benefits of downsizing, and even ways to make more money. There is a wealth of information, and by pursuing this dream, you're going to take a slice of it. Don't let your financial or credit status dissuade you from thinking there's no point in trying. After learning everything this book has to share, you will be amazed by the possibilities and options available. Even if it means only learning how to prepare for doing it in the future.

So, you may be wondering who this genius is that's going to miraculously make all of this happen. I'll tell you a secret: I'm not a genius, and there won't be a miracle. Just hard work, an open mind, and invaluable information based on years of experience. I bought my first home at age 23, right out of college. I understand the challenges many young people face when diving into the homeowner's market. After investing in real estate for the last seven years, I learned the dynamics well enough to feel that I needed to help others understand this as well so they could experience the same joy. Buying a home when you're so young is challenging, especially raising the down payment. But I learned that it's achievable, and this realization gave me a passionate desire to help others know how to buy a home and all I've learned about investing. All of the information and tools in this book are what I used in my journey to become such a young homeowner. I wasn't anyone different or special. I only learned the same as you can now.

The first step is being willing to go down this path. It has twists, switchbacks, hills, and pitfalls. It can be downright scary. At the same time, all of this is what makes it so exhilarating. Picture yourself sky-diving. Jumping off of a plane is absolutely terrifying, even when the coach is assuring you that the parachute will open. It's still that fear of the unknown, but when you land in one piece, all you can think about is how amazing you felt: the rush of adrenaline from the thrill of the fall and the absolute ecstasy of surviving it, since now you can proudly say that you did it. That's the same feeling in a homeowner's journey. However, you have the benefit of not being alone. Armed with this information, you will tackle this journey head-on with confidence. It isn't the same path for everyone, so before you take the first step, you'll learn the pieces of the real estate puzzle and how they tie in together. Only then can you understand where you fit into it and which path is right for you.

So as you look at that *For Sale* sign at what was once your home full of memories, take a deep breath and make a promise that you will never let this happen to you again. You are no longer simply a tenant dependent on the desires of your landlord. The time has come to change paths, step out of the rental rut, and onto the road of being a homeowner.

Chapter 1:

Crowdfunding Your Way to Homeownership

As you walk by the grocery store, you notice a bulletin board full of flyers, pamphlets, and business cards advocating for charities, small businesses, and services. You see a particular one advertising for a charity run with a small donation fee. It always feels good to give to charity, right? So you keep the flyer and plan your next Saturday to be a day of well-wishes and good charitable causes. But as you're driving home, you remember that it's no longer your home anymore, and you'd better start looking for a new one. It makes you wish you could do a charity run for a down payment. Believe it or not, you can, and it's possible through a highly-guarded business secret called crowdfunding.

Despite popular belief, raising money for a down payment can be done using the same tools that businesses and charities use. One of these is crowdfunding, which is the use of small amounts of capital from a large number of individuals to finance an idea and is often a business or a need. These individuals can be from a variety of sources, such as family, friends, customers, or independent investors. Not all of us are fortunate enough to have friends and family who are willing to give us a lump sum of cash, so crowdfunding is managed mainly online through social media or platforms designated solely to crowdfunding.

By using crowdfunding to source your down payment, you're essentially approaching it from a business finance standpoint, only doing the opposite of what is the traditional method. Traditionally, if a person wants to start a business and needs the capital to launch it, they would need to create a business plan, do some market research, create prototypes, and then pitch their idea to a limited number of wealthy individuals or companies. However, this is incredibly challenging and limiting since there are only a few key sources to approach, mainly being banks, angel investors, and venture capital firms. So a lot of the time, you're at a disadvantage for choice, and more often than not, it's simply time and money lost.

However, crowdfunding platforms have turned that traditional model on its head by allowing you as a single entrepreneur to showcase your idea to a much wider pool of investors. Instead of spending months sifting through the few choices you have and spending money doing it, you simply build your platform and let the investors come to you. There are also more ways for the parties to invest in your idea, from equity exchanges to small contributions for products or rewards. The benefits of crowdfunding are many due to the wider choice of investors and flexible options for fundraising. When you build a platform on an online crowdfunding source, you increase your capabilities to reach more potential investors, present your idea in a streamlined package, easily promote your idea through public relations and marketing, and be able to validate your idea since so many parties are seeing it and asking questions. This process is highly efficient and saves you the time and effort of pursuing each investor individually.

If it's this easy to source money for an idea or needs through public or private means, then you may wonder why you haven't heard of it before now. Simply put, this is because it was never identified under that term. However, the idea of using a crowd of people to fund a public or private need has been around since the 18th century. The history of crowdfunding can be a little tricky because of this. The concept has been around for centuries, but the term is still in its infancy, born out of the digital age. Not to mention the strategies have evolved and are still doing so, changing with times and technology.

The earliest forms of crowdfunding were used by Alexander Pope in 1713 and Mozart in 1783. Both men needed funds to finish their projects and appealed to the public to donate money in return for a reward. In Pope's case, it was a copy of the manuscript he wished to publish, where he used a "subscription method" to ask people to donate. Once they did, they would receive a copy of the published book. Mozart needed funds to perform three of his concertos and appealed to the public to help him by promising a personal thanks and mention of their names in the printed manuscripts. Neither of these examples were called crowdfunding at the time, but the seeds were planted that would bloom into an efficient, sophisticated tool for business finances.

Leaping forward to 1874, crowdfunding experienced its next stage of evolution and was used to reach the masses through the press. This was achieved by the Franco-American Union, a fundraiser used by America and France to raise funds for the Statue of Liberty. While France tried to raise funds to finish the statue, America attempted to raise funds to build the pedestal by appealing to the mass public through a man named Joseph Pulitzer, the publisher of the New York World. His appeal for this campaign was poignant and reached the hearts of many.

By 1962, visuals were being used for crowdfunding, where a crowdfunding campaign by the first Prime Minister of Independent India, Jawaharlal Nehru, was started when he used a visual to express the importance of contributions to the war against China. In 1976, the first form of community crowdfunding was born in India, and by 1996, the British rock band, Marillion, had brought it to the digital age. They laid the foundation for what is now the modern form of crowdfunding. Through online donations entirely on the internet, fans were able to contribute funds so that the band would not have to cancel its US tour. It was the pioneering moment for online crowdfunding.

In 2001, ArtistShare became the first website for crowdfunding, created by Brian Camelio, an American music producer and artist. He's arguably called the "father of crowdfunding" because he created the format that modern platforms use. This was quickly followed by the rising stars of 2008 to 2009, Indiegogo and Kickstarter. They were both online platforms designed to help fund entrepreneurs and initial start-ups using pre-sales. Though Kickstarter struggled to find its feet, the massive success of the company, Pebble, gave it new life in 2012. Pebble reached over $10 million in donations in one month for the pre-sale of its watches. The JOBS Act was also passed in 2012 by Barack Obama, which was another step in the evolution of crowdfunding. This allowed startups and businesses to find funds in exchange for equity and securities within their company and was considered a milestone moment for crowdfunding.

With this kind of history and success, you can see that it won't take long for crowdfunding to grow out of its relative infancy in the digital age and become even more popular as a means for business and entrepreneur ventures.

Types of Crowdfunding

When starting a business or campaign, there are always stages of growth throughout the process. Your venture is similar to raising a child. It will grow as you tend and nurture it. Depending at what stage your campaign is will determine what type of crowdfunding will work for you. It also varies depending on the type of product or service you have and your ultimate goal. There are four main types of crowdfunding: donation-based, rewards-based, equity-based, and debt-based. However, the three main types are donation, rewards, and equity.

How many times have we walked by a Salvation Army Santa at Christmas and dropped a few coins in the bucket for charity? We didn't think much about it, but what you just did was contribute to the Salvation Army's donation-based crowdfunding campaign. Donation-based crowdfunding is the type that is the most common. This is the one in which charities, fundraisers, and nonprofits work. It's so common that we run into it all the time and don't even notice what it is. Any campaign in which the investor or contributor receives no financial return is considered donation-based crowdfunding.

The sibling to this type of crowdfunding is the rewards-based type, since technically the investor or contributor is not receiving a financial or equity return. Instead, they will receive a form of your product or service as a reward in exchange for their contribution. This type of crowdfunding is mainly popular with online crowdfunding platforms since it allows the business owner to appeal for the contribution without compromising their finances or having to sell any part of their business.

Equity-based crowdfunding is the type in which the investor or contributor has the most to gain. Unlike donation-based and rewards-based, this type allows the investor to take a piece of ownership in your business by trading capital for equity shares. Since they are now a co-owner of the business, they will not only receive a financial return on their investment but will also receive a share of the profits through distribution or a dividend.

It's an attractive prospect for the investor but requires more loss from the business owner. However, if you don't mind sharing your business, it can be quite lucrative.

Knowing all of the crowdfunding methods is wonderful, but how do any of these apply for a down payment? Saving for a down payment isn't exactly a business venture, so it can be confusing to pinpoint which crowdfunding type works for your goal. The easiest type to go for is the donation-based kind, where you won't have to pay anything back to your investor. Unfortunately, this is very similar to getting money from friends and family. So the next alternative is to choose debt-based crowdfunding, where you will pay the money back on a predetermined agreement. This opens your options a bit wider since most people are willing to invest and help if they can be confident they'll get their money back. A creative approach is to use equity-based crowdfunding, depending on whether you're able to rent a part of your home or not. If so, you can give the proceeds of the rental back to the investors.

These options may make you ponder for a moment on whether or not this crowdfunding idea is a good one. However, when you look at the statistics of the success of first-time homebuyers, especially those 30 years old and under, you can see why this idea is starting to have merit. More than one out of 10 buyers state that saving for the down payment is the most difficult part of buying a home, and 30% of the millennial age group have reported experiencing the most trouble saving up the funds. Traditional methods used in the past often don't add up to the amount necessary, even when you're storing money away like a chipmunk in winter or borrowing from your retirement account if you're lucky enough to have one.

This is the reason you should consider crowdfunding as an alternative method and seek out platforms that are similar to Kickstarter and GoFundMe. There are platforms created specifically for people saving for a down payment, such as HomeFundMe, Down Payment Dreams, and Feather the Nest. Crowdfunding for your down payment can also be an easier way to reach the 20% goal that most need for a down payment, which will give you a lower interest rate and help you avoid paying for mortgage insurance. Technically, a first-time buyer only needs 10% for a down payment, but the more you can contribute to the purchase, the better off you'll be in the long run. Buying a home is one of the largest purchases in your life, so it's best to start right.

Though this idea for a down payment is in its infancy, it is gaining in popularity, mostly because people are living together well before they get married, and they tend to get married later on in life. Traditional gifts for the home are no longer necessary, and people would rather receive a contribution for a down payment for a home of their own. The other consideration to remember is that these donations are subject to gift guidelines. When purchasing a home through the lender, there will have to be gift letters stating the money received was a gift and not a loan. This is crucial since lenders will need to know where the source of this money came from. Some platforms do create their letters for the account creator stating the donations are gifts, but be aware that you obtain one. Every donation must be accounted for since lenders will reject an application if they feel the down payment is a loan. Check to see if your lender accepts gift letters, since not all do.

With online crowdfunding becoming more and more popular, it is hard to stand out. Many people are now asking for donations for a variety of reasons, and all of them seem as important as the other. When you're faced with emergency medical bills or helping an honor student attend college, the choices can seem vastly more important than your own. Gaining interest from friends and family is difficult, especially for something that could seem fairly material. So when you're trying to decide how to ask for donations, make sure you have a catchy selling point, such as my house is being sold out from under me.

If you're getting married, it's a perfect opportunity to transform wedding gifts into donations towards a down payment. In 2006, the online crowdfunding platform HoneyFund was created. Though it was originally designed for honeymoons, it has broadened its horizons and is now used from down payments to furniture. You even have the option to receive donations offline, by either the guests bringing it to the wedding or by mail, free of charge by HoneyFund. If you do decide to have the funds transferred directly into a PayPal account, there is a small fee.

However, before you get too overwhelmed, don't think that this world of online crowdfunding platforms is too difficult to navigate. There are ways to manage your campaign effectively, which we will explore next.

How to Raise Money

Have you ever sat in a math class and stared forlornly at an intimidatingly long algebraic equation? Beginning the process of crowdfunding can feel exactly like that math problem. It seems complicated, tedious, and frankly, you're not sure how to begin solving it. The entire concept of crowdfunding almost seems too good to be true, since it's getting your money from other people. However, though millions of people are doing it, if it were that easy, then everyone would be crowdfunding for anything they wanted. It takes skill, tenacity, and craftiness to make your crowdfunding campaign a success. Not to mention that the majority of people who even know of crowdfunding don't realize that it can be used for real estate purposes. It's been used mainly for other reasons, and real estate is the new kid on the block in this world. Fortunately, there is a formula similar to the one you'll use to solve that algebra equation.

The simplest way to start any process is to take one step at a time. By doing this, you're less likely to get overwhelmed and be tempted to drop the idea. The first step is to clearly define your goal. People want to understand the precise amount needed and the specific reason you need it. No one wants to donate to a cause that isn't clear, so it's best to start with knowing the exact amount you need, broken down into itemized sections if you can. For example, if you require a down payment of 20% for a house that costs $300,000, don't list it as such. That would be giving your potential contributors a math problem they don't want to solve. Instead, figure out that total yourself and list that instead. If you know that you only need 10% for the down payment and are asking for another 10% for furniture, state that as well. That way, you give your contributors a choice on which one they would rather help you with. People love the freedom of choice. The more choices you give them, the more willing they are to work with you.

Since online crowdfunding has been such a success over the years, there have been numerous platforms created, almost to the point that it's impossible to know of every single one. The good part is that each of these online platforms was designed for a particular niche, though there are still the ones that are for anything in general, such as GoFundMe (www.gofundme.com). However, your best odds at being successful is to choose one that fits your needs, especially for real estate. On mainstream crowdfunding sites, people aren't expecting requests for help for a down payment, and it may turn them off. But if you place yourself on a housing platform specifically designed for that, there won't be that element of surprise. Hatch My House (www.idopr.com/wedding/) is great for helping you itemize since you "build" your house, and your contributors can "buy" parts of it to help with either down payments, renovations, or even house decor. Or you can simply go to Down Payment Dreams (www.downpayment dreams.com) to simply request help for a down payment and nothing else. Another neat option is BoostUp, which incorporates a savings platform as well. This way, instead of asking for donations, contributors can simply match your savings dollar for dollar that you're adding to the account. Whichever site sounds best for you, it's best to remember a few key areas to watch out for in all of them. Try choosing the one with the lowest fees, both in platform fees and payment fees. It's also important that the website is easy to use and has an attractive design. Good customer support is essential, especially if you're new to creating and managing accounts. You'll also want to be sure that you have safe and quick access to your funds. And it's also nice to be able to share your fundraiser with others to get the word out, so be sure it has those capabilities as well.

Once you've achieved these first two steps, now is the time to sit down and have a heart-to-heart talk with yourself about why you're doing this. Part of creating your account is telling people your story, and this needs to be done honestly. There's no point in fabricating an outlandish story simply to pull at the heartstrings of potential investors, though not to say it hasn't been done. There's embellishing, and then there's just telling lies. Odds are good that you have a genuinely touching story for why you need help. If your landlord is selling the rental you've been living in for years, people will understand that you're in an unexpected situation you had no control over. If you're not a natural storyteller, even explaining your situation can be difficult, so there are a few questions to ask yourself that can help. Starting with the basic who, what, when, where, how, and why questions can help get the ball rolling, but there are even more specific questions than those, such as what will the funds be used for? How are you connected to this cause? What will the donations be used for? And the most important one to ask is why do you need this donation? The "why" question is imperative. This is the question that makes people interested and feel emotionally connected to the cause. Once you've got your story, top it off with a strong title that encompasses your issue and will catch the eye of the reader.

This next step may seem a bit contradictory since chances are you're using a crowdfunding site so that you don't have to ask your friends and family for help, but it's beneficial. When you've created your fundraiser, share it with those closest to you and ask them to critique it. Ask for suggestions for refining the story or even the layout. Hearing these suggestions can help improve your campaign in ways you couldn't see, and it opens the door for the opportunity for them to donate. But even if they don't offer, ask them for a small one, even if it's simply five dollars. The reason for this is that potential contributors are more willing to donate if they've seen that someone else has already. Your aunt may not be able to help you with enough for the down payment, but she would probably be willing to donate a dollar or two to help get your campaign off the ground. Once you've gotten enough small donations from friends and family, you can start sharing your fundraiser everywhere, be it through social media or by putting flyers up on local bulletin boards.

Show Appreciation

Never forget to show appreciation to your contributors. If you've been fortunate enough to have people donate to your cause, then they deserve tokens of gratitude, and those can be as simple as a thank you letter. Anything that lets them know you're thinking of them and keeping them a part of your story. Ideally, you want to strengthen relationships with your contributors, which leads us to the next step. It's important to keep your contributors updated on your progress and story. That can be a little tricky with down payments, since the money usually has to be saved up for quite a long time before anyone sees you moving into a house. In this case, it's even more important for you to keep them updated on your plans and how the process is going so that you don't cause ill-wished gossip about what you're doing with the money instead.

Understand the Costs

Last but not least is to understand the costs. Nothing ever comes for free, and as convenient and nice as the crowdfunding platforms are, they do have a price. These sites will take a percentage, usually between five to six percent, of each donation. Obviously, it's best if you can get cash, but since that's not always an option, it's good to calculate the costs before starting. You should also check with an accountant before starting to make sure that you won't owe any taxes on the donations.

Crowdfunding doesn't have to be hard or overwhelming if taken one step at a time and always keeping the "why" for your goal in mind. There are many niche sites for funding down payments, such as Homefundit (www.homefundit.com/en). So go set up your site and tip your toe into the crowdfunding pool!

Chapter 2:
Build a Line of Credit

The shopping mall is bustling with people, and you're having a great time shopping with your friend. You see an item you'd love to buy, but you know you don't have the money in your bank account to afford it. Without thinking, you whip out your credit card and purchase the item, knowing you can pay for it later. People use credit cards daily without a thought, and yet when faced with needing a large sum of money, they don't think about credit at all. Businesses have been using credit lines for years now to sustain their working capital needs or grab strategic opportunities, but people have yet to grasp the concept. This could be because banks don't like to advertise lines of credit, and it does take some time to build one.

Also referred to as a LOC, a line of credit is a pre-set borrowing limit that you can use at any time and is an arrangement made between a bank and a client. A maximum loan amount is established that the client can borrow, and the borrower can withdraw as much as they need until the limit is reached. If it's an open line of credit, the money can be repaid and borrowed again repeatedly. An open line of credit is a form of revolving account due to the never-ending cycle of spending money, paying it back, and spending it again. These kinds of accounts are different from the installment loans you'll find for mortgages and car loans. Unlike with a credit card, interest is only charged when you borrow, not while the line of credit is open. The bank decides the amount of interest and payment amounts. Depending on the line of credit, some allow you to write checks, while others have a type of credit or debit card. One of the nicest advantages of a line of credit is the built-in flexibility it has. You can request a certain amount, but you don't need to use it all at once. Borrowers can also adjust their repayment amounts based on their capabilities and can choose between paying the balance in full or monthly installments.

A line of credit is a kind of open-ended loan that doesn't charge interest unless you take from it, and even then, it only charges interest on the amount you withdrew. For example, you go to the bank and ask to apply for an open line of credit. The bank approves you and tells you the amount you're allowed to spend. Now, let's assume that amount is $20,000, but you don't need it all right now. You simply withdraw the amount you need, and the interest then starts to accrue. This is when you need to make at least the minimum payments, which will be added back to your account as you pay them.

Having better credit scores can help you qualify for a lower annual percentage rate, and some credit lines may come with annual fees and borrowing amount limits. Once you've qualified for the credit line, a set time frame, known as the "draw period," begins. This period is when you can draw money from the account and usually lasts for several years. Once the draw period ends, however, you start the repayment period, which is a set time to repay the remaining balance without any access to more money. Keep in mind that having a line of credit does affect your credit score, and using a lot of the balance or making late payments will have a negative effect on them.

If opening a line of credit appeals to you, it's a simple matter of going to your bank and applying for one. However, there are a few tips to learn before heading over to the local bank. First, check to make sure your credit scores are healthy, and if not, make some changes to improve them so that you can increase your chances of qualifying for a lower interest rate. Next, come up with a plan on how much money you need and how you plan to spend it. You want to make sure that you're not applying for this line of credit for the wrong reasons, because in the long run, that could do more harm than good.

Lines of credits can be quite beneficial, but you must be sure they work best for your situation. If you have an unstable income, or deep down the honest part of yourself knows you can't make payments, a line of credit is not appropriate. Defaulting on payments will lower your credit score, and if it's a secured line with collateral, you may lose possession of that collateral. Also, lines of credit don't always have better interest rates than personal loans if you don't have any collateral to use. Depending on your credit, an unsecured personal loan might be a better option. They're also not appropriate if you're going to use the money for short-term needs, such as a vacation, because that simply means you're not in the financial position to get into new debt.

The most appropriate times to use a line of credit are when you have a large home improvement project, education costs, or another kind of major expense, and you know that you have the income to make steady repayments. These reasons are best done with a secured line of credit or a HELOC. This has another benefit since a HELOC can be tax-deductible. Another appropriate use for them is if you have several small debts that you're paying off. Consolidating them into one unsecured line of credit can possibly lower the annual percentage rate and make it one payment instead of several. Depending on your credit health and the line of credit terms, this can be done without collateral.

Getting a line of credit is a fairly straightforward process, and depending on your situation and the need you have for it, it could be beneficial. Lines of credits are based on several factors such as household income, your ability to repay, your credit score and history, and specific other factors such as home value or study program if you're looking to apply for a home equity line or student line of credit. There are two main differences between lines of credit, as we've briefly touched upon here already, and those are secured and unsecured credit lines.

Secured vs. Unsecured

If a friend asked to borrow money from you, your first thought might be how will I get my money back, depending on the trustworthiness of that friend. There's always a risk with loaning money, and sometimes we even know we won't see it again when we do.

Banks, however, like to have guarantees when given the opportunity. And if they can't get a guarantee, they will draw up agreements that will still get their money back in the long term. We typically can't do this with family or friends, but financial institutions want to cover themselves. This is why there are two main differences between secured lines of credit and unsecured lines of credit. It's based on your creditworthiness and what asset you have to offer. Both types are good, but each has an advantage and disadvantage.

A secured line of credit means that you're putting forth collateral to "secure" the loan. This makes the loan more secure since the bank can seize the collateral if you default on your payments by putting a lien on it and legally obtaining it that way. Once acquired, they can sell the collateral to get their money back. Lenders prefer secured lines of credit since they're lower-risk, so interest rates and fees are more affordable. Common examples of secured loans are mortgage and auto loans. These are high-value items that are worth good collateral, so banks are more willing to approve loans since they can take the house or car and sell it for lots of money if the payments default. Since the bank has a form of guarantee for getting their money, secured lines of credit often have higher credit limits as well. These are all advantages of having a secured line of credit, but another one is that the collateral generally cushions any poor credit you may have. If your credit score is less than admirable, banks will feel more comfortable if you have a bargaining chip, like a car or house.

Despite this sounding like a good arrangement, there are disadvantages of secured lines of credit in which to be aware. The first is that unless you have a high-valued asset to offer as collateral, a secured line of credit won't work for you, so it is fairly limiting when choosing it for something personal like a down payment. Also, as much as it sounds nice, a higher line of credit amount will increase the risk of getting into more debt. People like to spend as much as they make because it's so easy to do. If the bank hands you $60,000, odds are pretty good you'll find a way to spend that money since it's available to you. Be cautious when given a higher credit line since it can be potentially harmful to your debt to income ratio. The reason banks prefer secured lines of credit is that you inherit all the risk. It may be easy to have good intentions when you acquire the credit, but bear in mind the risk you're putting your valuable asset in. There's no point in using a line of credit to get a house if you won't be able to make the payments. You'll end up losing the house anyway. It's important to carefully study the terms of the agreement and understand the contract before you sign. The lower interest rates and higher credit amounts still make the secured line of credit more preferable, but there are key factors to consider before placing your assets at risk.

Opposite to the secured line is the unsecured line of credit, which is entirely different mainly because the bank inherits all the risk this time since you don't have any collateral to offer. If you stop making payments, the bank doesn't have many ways to recover the loss. However, they can take legal action against you, such as hiring a debt collector or charging you with a lawsuit and taking you to court. Your credit will also suffer since they will report your defaulted debts or late payments to the credit bureaus. Banks don't like taking risks, so, understandably, unsecured lines of credit are a bit more difficult to obtain for both businesses and individuals. A good example of an unsecured line of credit is a credit card, which is why many of them have very high interest rates. Businesses can be approved for unsecured lines of credit, but generally only if they are well-established and have an excellent reputation, since the repayments are dependent on the future income of the business.

One of the main advantages of an unsecured line of credit is that the borrower doesn't have all the risk. There's nothing valuable set against the loan that the bank can take from you if you default payments. And you can be approved for an unsecured line of credit without having to own collateral, which is perfect for someone who doesn't own anything of high value. They also generally have open-ended contracts without an end date, so there's less pressure to get the payments paid in full on time. Another advantage is for businesses who are worried they might have cash crunches in the near future since an open-ended credit line is useful for that.

All of these need to be weighed against the disadvantages. Banks are more nervous about this kind, so interest rates and fees are going to be higher, meaning more money is paid in the long term. Because of this risk, banks won't want to give as much since that means they could potentially lose more, so credit amounts you can borrow will be lower. This is important to consider if you know that you need a high amount since your odds are less likely to get it this way. They're also harder to be approved for since, once again, the banks don't like to take risks. It also causes them to monitor the activity of your credit score, cash flow, and other factors more carefully.

Since both unsecured and secured lines of credit have their pros and cons, it can sometimes be hard to decide which one best suits your purpose. It all depends on how you plan to use the money. If it's day-to-day purchases, an unsecured line of credit will be more beneficial since your expenditures will be minimal, and an open-end account can be convenient. However, if you need a large lump of cash for a big project or down payment, it may not be your best option since it has higher interest rates. Since you know the exact amount of money you need, an open-end account won't matter, and you can benefit from the lower interest rates and ease of applying.

Either way, both secured and unsecured lines of credit have good advantages over other kinds of loans. They're both flexible and can be used repeatedly when needed, often with low minimum payments and no end dates to pay in full as long as the payments are current. Just keep in mind why you're borrowing the money and weigh the pros and cons carefully.

Types of Credit

While you're weighing the advantages and disadvantages of both secured and unsecured lines of credit, it's useful to know that each kind has a different type. Being secured or unsecured is simply explaining the terms in which the credit line is agreed. But there are three types of credit lines that are specific to a person's needs. These are personal lines of credit, home equity lines of credit, or HELOC, and business lines of credit. Each type of credit line is secured or unsecured and has different requirements to be eligible for them. This information will allow you to narrow your search and get more specific in what you're searching for.

We'll start with a personal line of credit. This type of credit is a flexible, revolving line of credit since they can continually draw from their credit limit over a set period as long as payments are current. The banks lend a set amount of money for an agreed amount of time, which is usually several years. Then you can access these funds repeatedly during the draw period. Once paid back, the funds are available to draw from again. This is a great option for someone who is looking at needing large sums of money over some time, such as during home improvements or a child attending college. However, it is important to note that personal lines of credit are usually unsecured, and though you won't need collateral, some qualifications must be met. These are generally dependent on your income level, credit history, and outgoing expenses, along with possible additional fees. They also like to see a credit score of at least 680 or higher. The kinds of fees to be aware of when searching for personal lines of credit are annual fees, which can be charged annually or broken into monthly payments, late fees on delinquent payments, and small transaction fees on withdrawals. Interest rates on personal lines of credit tend to be variable, but some financial institutions offer them at low fixed rates, which are useful if you need to do a consolidation with other loans you have. You also want to check to see if there are any origination fees, maintenance fees, or prepayment fees for the life of the loan.

A home equity line of credit, or HELOC, is the traditional example of a secured line of credit. This type is almost self-explanatory and works much the same as a personal line of credit in that it offers a set amount of funds during a draw period, which is usually around ten years. The difference, however, is that your house is the collateral. To even be eligible for a HELOC, a home would need to be set as collateral to be approved. Generally, the amount of credit you are approved for depends on the amount of equity available in the home, not the house's value itself. The approval amount typically falls around 80 percent of your home's value minus the balance still owed on your mortgage. Similar to the personal line of credit, interest and monthly payments are only charged when the first withdrawal is made. However, there are closing costs to this line of credit, much like when during a property appraisal. Since this line of credit is dependent on the amount of equity in your home, it's good to consider the maximum loan amount for which you would be eligible. If you don't have much equity, then a personal line of credit may help you borrow a higher amount. HELOCs also tend to have variable interest rates, which can fluctuate throughout the loan's period, though these tend to be lower interest rates. One benefit of a HELOC is if you're using it for a home improvement project since it can then be tax-deductible. Interest can be deducted from the loan if the money used is to purchase, build, or vastly improve the house used for collateral. These are great lines of credit for higher expenses or to consolidate high-interest debt.

The third type of credit is a business line of credit. It differs from the other two since it doesn't have a fixed loan amount, but rather the borrower takes the money as needed. All of your eligibility is reliant on your business. The bank will review your business's profits, market value, and the business risks it has inherited before deciding on any loan details. This type can be very convenient for business owners due to its speed and flexibility. Once approved, the borrower can withdraw funds whenever necessary instead of waiting for approval on a set amount each time a purchase is required. It's also flexible and can be used for anything, including services, as long as it's relevant for maintaining the business.

Knowing how and when to use lines of credit can be very beneficial, but you can also harness this information and focus it towards a down payment on your first home. The best way is by obtaining a credit line for yourself and your partner, if applicable. If you're fortunate enough to have a friend or family member working at a financial institution, approach them and ask them to lend you the amount. The reason for this is because employees are given lines of credit at much lower interest rates. Sign an agreement to repay the money plus the interest rate after the time that the down payment sits in your bank has lapsed. It's also beneficial to compare lender's interest rates and to make sure you understand all of the associated fees. Just as important is to understand the difference between the draw and repayment periods. When applying for a home equity line of credit, be aware of a "minimum draw" that the lender may mention. You can also research testimonials of each lender to see what past experiences others have had with them. Searching the bank's website or requesting referrals from the bank personally can work, but it also helps if you search within your network of people or other online resources. At the same time, a bank's customer service values also hold significant importance since you could potentially be dealing with them for years.

All of this information can be daunting, but by dissecting the facts of each type of credit line and the best uses for it, you can target the exact needs you require and how best to implement them. Remember, lines of credit have been tools businesses have used for years, and for a good reason. Though people are only recently becoming aware of their potential, it's important to use them wisely and educate yourself on their pros and cons. If you know you're a shopaholic with low self-control, a revolving, open-end account may not work for you, so perhaps a closed-end one would be safer. Knowing yourself as an individual as well as the requirements for each loan can help you make the most suitable match.

Chapter 3:

Consider 100% Financing: The USDA Home Loan

When trying to find a way to buy a home, the words one hundred percent financing may sound too good to be true. But in the case of the USDA Home Loan, they're bonafide solid gold. These loans have been around since 1949 and have made millions of fortunate Americans into homeowners. You may be wondering why you haven't heard about something like this before since it sounds so incredible. The fact is that these loans were designed by the U.S. Department of Agriculture to improve the economy of rural America, so it doesn't suit all types of buyers. If your job forces you to live in the middle of a city, this option won't work for you. However, if you can look further afield, and that may mean literally, then you're in luck and might be able to take advantage of the benefits that this loan can offer you.

Let's start with knowing precisely what a USDA Home Loan is. These loans are a government-sponsored mortgage-assisted program for people looking to buy a rural home, though some suburban areas are also acceptable. They're mainly designed for borrowers who are considered low-income and don't have high enough credit scores to qualify for a traditional mortgage. Issued through the USDA Rural Development Guaranteed Housing Loan Program, they come with zero down payment and low-interest benefits. This program is designated to certain areas that cover several rural and suburban locations. By helping people purchase homes, this program saved the economy and helped improve the quality of life for many in the small, forgotten towns of rural America. In 2017 alone, the USDA managed to help 127,000 families buy or upgrade their homes.

Though not specifically created for first-time buyers, the USDA loan can be very helpful since they don't require a down payment. This is especially beneficial for the first-time buyers without high incomes, such as college graduates who haven't climbed the corporate ladders yet, or newlyweds who still have wedding debt. When learning how these loans work, you'll be able to see how first-time buyers can make the most out of the opportunity.

Every year, the USDA helps support thousands of families into homes. It can be easy to see the temptation to move rural with interest rates that can be as low as one percent, and in general, a credit score doesn't need to be any higher than 640 to be approved. Even the monthly repayments are designed to work around a low-income, not being able to exceed more than 29 percent of your monthly income, with other monthly payments not being able to exceed 41 percent of your monthly income. However, before you convince yourself that you love that little house on the prairie, there are some facts to consider.

The way these loans work can be fairly restrictive, so you have to be aware of the criteria to see if it fits you. Your household income must be at or below the low-income limit set by the government for the area in which you want to buy a home, and you have to be willing to embrace rural life. Fortunately, the USDA does have a broad definition of "rural," so some suburban areas in or near major cities are allowed. Surprisingly enough, USDA loans are not directly offered by the USDA but by traditional lenders like banks. The only difference is that the

USDA backs these loans, meaning the federal government will cover a part of the mortgage if the borrower defaults. This is why it's much easier to be approved for a USDA loan than a traditional one since banks have a guarantee.

There are three different types of USDA loans: Guaranteed, Direct, and USDA Home Improvement. Each type works in a different way and for a specific purpose. Knowing these types can help you determine which category suits you best.

The Guaranteed USDA loan works similar to how we just explained. The borrower applies through a local bank that is partnered with the USDA so that the mortgage will be partly covered if the borrower defaults. They can also be used to build a new home or refinance a pre-existing guaranteed loan that the borrower has. This is the loan that most low-income and low credit score borrowers will benefit from since the bank is more flexible in approving them. It also suits these types of borrowers best since it doesn't require a down payment. However, a yearly "guarantee" fee is additional but is worked into your monthly payments. These loans can be as much as 100 percent of the home's appraisal value, but if the sale price is less than that, the buyer can use the remainder to pay for repairs, set up utilities, or cover closing costs. Though the bank can decide which low-interest rate they want, they are required to make it a fixed rate for a 30-year term.

For a Direct USDA loan, the USDA becomes the lender for the buyer directly through the Single Family Housing Guaranteed Loan Program, and covers existing homes and the costs of repairing or improving a home. This is usually only for low-income to very low-income families who are unable to be approved for any other type of financing for a residence. To qualify for this type of loan, the borrower's income must be equal to or below the low-income limit in a specific area. In some areas, this limit can fall below $17,000. Not only do you not have to pay for a down payment, but you won't have to pay for mortgage insurance either. The interest rates are fixed but determined by market rates. Borrowers can apply for payment assistance which would make the rate as low as one percent. These types of loans are usually for 33 years but can go as long as 38 years, depending on the borrower's income level. This type of loan will not cover a home that is considered unusually large or valuable for its area or one that's going to be used as a business or to generate income.

The third type of loan is the Home Improvement USDA loan and is strictly for repairing or improving the home for low-income borrowers. These reasons can be for updating the home, necessary repairs, or eliminating health and safety hazards. The borrower can also use them to install or fix heating systems, new roofs, or insulate the home. Loan amounts cannot exceed $20,000, and the borrower will have 20 years to repay the loan with a low fixed interest rate of one percent for the life of the loan. If you're at least 62 years old and don't have the income to repay the loan, the program will have grants available to cover it.

Whichever circumstance you're in, if you're able or willing to live in a rural area and have a low income, then a USDA loan may be the right option for you.

How to Qualify

If living in the wide-open space of the countryside is sounding more appealing, then it's best to know if you're eligible for a USDA loan. We've briefly touched upon a few key areas in which USDA loans work that suggest what you need to qualify, such as choosing a house in a designated rural area and having a low income. But, of course, it isn't that simple. This is a government-backed loan, so there must be more criteria and small print to it. We'll explore all the fine details and make sure you understand the process in its entirety to see if this option will still work.

The USDA has created basic eligibility requirements that cover credit, income, home location, and property usage. These are the barebone facts that you must meet to even begin the process. Minimum qualifications include being a United States citizen or legal permanent resident, the ability to prove creditworthiness, a stable income, and a willingness to repay the mortgage with at least 12 months of no late payments; your adjusted household income is at least 115 percent of the area's median income, and the property will serve as a primary residence in a rural area. All of these factors play a significant role in the success of your application. It sounds fairly straightforward, but it's important to study each factor in detail. In addition to these, each bank or lender may also add its own internal guidelines and requirements.

Despite it being said that a minimum credit score of 640 is necessary, there is technically no minimum credit score requirement to qualify for a USDA loan. However, if you have a credit score of 640 or higher, you will qualify for the USDA's automated underwriting system, which can make the process easier and less strict. So although having a credit score lower than 640 still makes you eligible, they have to undergo manual underwriting, which means harsher guidelines. Therefore, the process is much simpler if you can prove creditworthiness. To prove this to the bank, they will review criteria such as your credit score, any repayment patterns you've made in the past, credit utilization, and your length of credit history. If you haven't established any credit history, you may still be eligible, but credit verification will be in the form of rent, utility, or insurance payments as alternatives.

Verifying income can be a bit more complicated than simply checking your pay stubs and bank account statement. Throughout the application process, the USDA will check four different income calculations to determine income eligibility. These are your annual household income, adjusted annual household income, the USDA qualifying income, and repayment income. It can be hard to believe that one person's income can be divided into so many categories, but there are different factors for each. Minimally, you must have a stable income that can be verified and is likely to continue. This is usually done by the bank, which will request two years' worth of income tax returns and pay stubs to make sure you have dependable employment. Oftentimes, we don't understand the differences between each type of income. Knowing this before applying can help you be more prepared.

Many people can get confused by annual and adjusted annual, thinking they're similar. Though they are related, they're used for different reasons. Your annual household income is the total projected income of the adult members in your household. This means that every adult occupant's income will be counted towards the household's income limit, whether they are part of the loan or not. The adjusted annual household income is taking the amount of the annual household income and subtracting all acceptable deductions from it. This is used to determine whether or not you meet the program's income restrictions.

To ensure that the applicant is within the low to moderate income group for the program, the USDA sets a maximum benchmark for the amount of adjusted annual household income a household can have at the time of the application. They set amounts of income, which are the USDA qualifying incomes, that are acceptable. The general USDA set incomes are simple. For households with one to four members, the income is $91,900, and for households with five to eight members, the income is $121,300. The USDA adjusts for regional differences by varying income limits with household size and location. They use a base income limit that's set to 115 percent of the area's median household income and then compare your total qualifying income to the regional median to determine eligibility.

Though still considered in the income category, repayment income is entirely different from qualifying income. While the qualifying income is to make sure the borrower's income matches the eligibility requirements, repayment income is to ensure that the borrower's income can make the repayments. Normally, a bank will assess an applicant's creditworthiness with a debt-to-income ratio. The USDA set a 41 percent ratio for USDA loans, meaning that you cannot spend more than 41% of your monthly income on debt. If you're spending more than 41% per month on debt, it is still possible to be eligible, but there will be tougher restrictions on your application.

As you can see, verifying income is a large, involved part of the application process. However, it doesn't end there. Aside from income, there are also loan location and loan property requirements. We already know that the property must be in a rural location. However, understanding the USDA's broad definition of rural is critical when choosing a home. According to the USDA, a rural location is defined as open country that is not part of an urban area. The required population could be up to 35,000, depending on the designated area. This definition of rural makes up around 97% of the nation's land that would be eligible for a USDA loan. So don't feel like you have to be completely on the outskirts of nowhere quite yet! Unless this is what you desire.

The USDA's goal for this program was to provide safe and sanitary housing for low-income households. This is why they set basic property requirements that protect home buyers and lenders. These requirements are that the home must be the buyer's primary residence, it must have direct access to a street, road, or driveway, and it must have adequate utility services, such as water and waste disposal. As mentioned before, the property can also not be used to generate income. However, if it is an unused farming residence with silos, barns, commercial greenhouses, and livestock facilities and is no longer used for commercial reasons, that property would still be eligible. Other examples of eligible properties include short sale and foreclosed homes, manufactured or modular homes, condos or townhouses, and newly constructed homes.

Earlier on, we mentioned that USDA loans often require mortgage insurance. The reason behind this is that since these loans are guaranteed by the USDA, this program is partially funded. But to keep the program running, they have to charge mortgage insurance premiums to the homeowner. There are two mortgage insurance costs, upfront and monthly. However, as of 2016, the USDA lowered the rates so that for purchases and refinancing, it's a 1% upfront fee, and for all other loans, it's a 0.35% annual fee, based on the remaining principal balance each year. Mortgage insurance is not paid in cash but added to the loan balance so you can pay over time.

These types of loans have helped millions of people find a way to achieve their dream of homeownership, but as with most loans, there are advantages and disadvantages. Weighing the pros and cons can help you determine whether you're stepping into a goldmine or a minefield.

The Pros and Cons

Between conventional loans and government programs, there is a vast range of options for potential home buyers. It's not only overwhelming but possible to get trapped in the quagmire of facts about each of them that it becomes impossible to make a decision. However, we will cover the list of pros and cons about a USDA loan that is simple and easy to understand to help you wade through the sea of choices.

The first and most obvious advantage of a USDA loan is that it doesn't require any down payment. Zero money upfront attracts a lot of home buyers, especially those buying for the first time. Aside from a VA loan, the USDA loan is the only other program that offers this advantage. So if saving money is an issue for you, this could save you years of painstaking hardship of putting money aside.

Where conventional loans require a minimum credit score of 720, the USDA loan doesn't have a minimum credit score requirement. As mentioned, it can benefit you if you have a score of 640 or higher, so you can take advantage of the automated underwriting system, but for those with little to no credit history, this loan may be your only option. Especially if you're young and haven't had time to build up lots of credit history. The USDA even utilizes its own internal underwriting system to qualify loans. This can be beneficial for those with poor credit that would scare off traditional lenders. In using their system, the USDA allows for more flexibility in reviewing the borrower's qualifications so that they can help you as much as possible.

Origination fees can often be a surprise to home buyers when they must pay them upfront. Depending on the type of loan, this fee can vary, but with USDA loans, buyers pay a guaranteed 2% fee of the total loan amount. And unlike other loans, this fee is not paid upfront but rolled into the total mortgage amount to be paid over time.

It also can't be beaten for insurance rates. The USDA loan has the lowest insurance rates out of all the mortgage loans.

Though the rates will vary due to the lender you choose, they will still be lower than most market rates and can even be improved if you have a good credit score, a low debt-to-income ratio, and can put some money down as a down payment. But even if none of these apply to you, this advantage can give you an interest rate that's as low as someone who has excellent credit.

Another added benefit is that if you wish to refinance in the future to lower your monthly payments or get a better interest rate, the USDA's streamlined refinancing process is simple and efficient. It can take as little as three weeks to process, and it doesn't require credit reports, a home appraisal, or a property inspection. The refinance will simply go into another USDA loan.

USDA loans are also always in common fixed-rate 15 to 30-year mortgages. You can also own property and still apply for a USDA loan, as long as that other property was not financed through the USDA. These advantages can certainly make you excited, but before your glasses become too rose-colored, let's take a look at the disadvantages of one.

The most immediate disadvantage is, of course, the fact that these loans are geographically restricted. If you want to live in an area with a population of 35,000 or more or want a property that produces income, then the requirements for this loan could be a severe drawback. Many people must live in a city to be near work, or those who want to run a business.

For those picturing a nice vacation cabin out in the woods, there's bad news. The potential home must also be only for a single-family residence, not a vacation home or secondary property. The USDA loan is not to be used for multi-family residences, so if you're needing a loan for multi-family, other options might be more suitable.

These loans can also be restrictive for those with professional salaries since there are stringent income limits set. USDA loans are solely designed for low to moderate incomes depending on the county in which they live. If your income is above that level, you will not be eligible.

Many people with low incomes and poor credit see the USDA's upfront fee as a small price to pay for being able to purchase a home, but it can be a disadvantage compared to other loans. Though this fee can be rolled into the mortgage amount, it can be up to several thousand dollars, depending on the loan amount. You can weigh this against not having to come up with a down payment, but it's important to keep in mind the total amount of your loan.

Rates with USDA loans must be fixed and are never allowed to be adjustable. At the moment, that's perfectly fine since fixed rates are low, but if rates changed, you wouldn't have an adjustable-rate option to take advantage of it. Some may argue that this is a disadvantage since fixed rates are arguably preferable, but it can be helpful to take note of this.

Refinancing also comes with some restrictions, despite the streamlined process the USDA offers. There are no cash-out refinances allowed. A cash-out refinance is a type of loan that lets you receive cash if there's equity built into the home. Though you will be allowed to refinance, you're not allowed to receive cash. Also, to qualify for refinancing, you must have made 12 consecutive mortgage payments on time, and the home must be your primary residence. Refinancing is also limited to 30-year loans and is not available in every state.

A commonly asked question is if there's a maximum sales price allowed for the home. The answer is a simple no. There is no loan or sale price maximum. However, the maximum housing expense, which is the monthly mortgage payment with tax and insurance, is generally 30% of the buyer's gross monthly income.

Both the pros and cons of a USDA home loan can be weighed equally, but the fact that it has benefited millions stays the same.

Chapter 4:

Poor Credit Score? No Worries; Take an FHA Loan

Buyers with low incomes and poor credit scores who can't or don't want to live out in the country, or need to purchase a home outside of the USDA's guidelines, don't have to give up hope. There is another loan option out there for you, and it's called the FHA loan. These loans are also beneficial for those who cannot afford a down payment that's large enough to suit a conventional loan.

The FHA loan is an insured mortgage by the Federal Housing Administration. So it's another type of government-backed loan that is also designed for low to moderate-income borrowers with poor credit. This loan is especially beneficial for first-time buyers with weak credit scores or no established credit. You will need to provide some down payment since the FHA loan will fund only up to 96.5% of the home's value, but this down payment percentage is drastically lower than the 20% required for a conventional mortgage and can be as low as 3.5%. Unique advantages of the FHA loans are that you're allowed to purchase not only single-family residences, but also condos, multi-unit properties, or manufactured homes as well. Borrowers can also get funding for renovations and repairs through the FHA 203(k) program and can use gift money or assistance from the seller to fund the down payment.

So who is the Federal Housing Administration? Many people who are only aware of traditional mortgage options have most likely never heard of them. The Federal Housing Administration was established during the Great Depression and stock market crash in the 1930s to solve the widespread foreclosures, defaults, and bankruptcies that plagued the nation during that time. They ensured that banks and mortgage brokers would receive some form of repayment guarantee. By backing people's loans, they could create a way for large numbers of people who had lost everything to buy homes once again and stimulate the housing market while also ensuring some stability for the banks. Making the loans affordable and easier to obtain gave more people this opportunity.

Today, the Federal Housing Administration still guarantees these loans to lenders on the borrower's behalf. If the borrower defaults on payments, the FHA will accept responsibility to repay the debt. The borrower is still obligated to make payments, but lenders are more willing to be flexible with their terms by having this guarantee.

If you have a way to offer some down payment but are unable to get accepted through traditional means because of credit or income, this chapter will help guide you through the process of understanding the FHA loan.

Understanding the FHA

In many ways, the FHA loan works the same as any government-insured loan. They have easier guidelines for credit as well as low closing costs and down payment requirements. They also come in 15 to 30-year mortgage terms with fixed interest rates. So what sets them apart?

The flexible underwriting standards that the FHA implements are what allow borrowers to purchase a home without good credit or high income and savings. However, FHA loans work by charging you mortgage insurance to protect the lender if the loan defaults. All loans where you put down less than 20% for the down payment are subjected to mortgage insurance. FHA loans have two mortgage insurance premiums that you must pay. The first is the upfront mortgage insurance, which is 1.75% of the loan amount, and that must be paid when you are approved for the loan. However, this can be added to the loan as well. The second is annual mortgage insurance, and this can range from 0.45% to 1.05% of the loan amount and loan-to-value ratio, depending on whether the mortgage is 15 or 30 years. This premium is automatically rolled into your monthly payments for the year.

This may all sound familiar since it's similar to the USDA loan, but there are key differences. Mortgage insurance premiums with FHA loans are canceled after 11 years if you were able to finance 90% or less of the home's value and maintain current payments. However, if your loan-to-value ratio was greater than 90%, you will have to carry the mortgage insurance until the loan is paid fully. Despite having to pay for two mortgage insurance premiums, FHA loans are popular with first-time buyers or those with low to moderate-income levels. You can even apply again for another home, as long as it will be a primary residence.

To obtain an FHA loan, you don't go to the FHA itself but rather find FHA-approved lenders. The FHA simply insures the loan, but the lender finances it. These lenders can be from a variety of sources, such as large bank firms and credit unions, to small community banks or independent mortgage lenders. Each type of lender has different costs, rates, and underwriting standards, so it's important to compare several and see which one suits you. Important factors to look for is a lender who is competent and will close the loan without charging you lots of money and who doesn't have rates that are higher than the market rate.

There are loan limits with an FHA loan, but as of 2021, these limits have been raised and are quite generous. The new floor limit for single-family residences is now $356,362, and the new ceiling limit for high-cost areas is $822,375. Floor limits are the minimum amount, and the ceiling limits are the maximum amounts that the FHA will insure. Keep a sharp eye on these limits since the FHA updates them every year due to changing home prices. Loan limits are set by the Federal Housing Finance Agency, and the FHA is required by law to adjust its amounts based on these limits. They can also vary according to the cost of living in a certain area, even as specific as one county to the next. There are exceptions made for residences in Alaska, Hawaii, Guam, and the Virgin Islands since home construction in these locations is more expensive.

One of the main reasons this loan is so popular with first-time buyers is due to the low down payment and ability to use gift funds as a down payment. Gift funds can be used for 100% of the down payment and closing costs, but credit cards or other unsecured loans cannot. Down payments can be as low as 3.5% with a minimum credit score of 580. Closing costs can also be added to the loan, preventing you from needing much cash. FHA loans can be used for repeat buyers but normally aren't due to the buyer being able to use the sale of their home as a down payment for the next.

Another key attraction for this loan is the incredibly low mortgage rates. They're one of the lowest mortgage rates you can find, though you must remember to balance this with the fact that you need to pay mortgage insurance. Fixed 30-year mortgage rates tend to be around 3.25%, while variable, 30-year mortgage rates are around 3.75%. These low rates make it easier to qualify for an FHA since any reduction in monthly payment can help your debt-to-income ratio. However, the annual percentage rates, or APR, can be high, which is why many people refinance later if they have sufficient equity.

There are several requirements to qualify for an FHA loan. However, there is a difference between what the FHA requires and individual lenders. We will cover the minimum FHA requirements, but be sure to check with your chosen lender what theirs will be.

Though a credit score of 580 is required to be able to pay a 3.5% down payment, lower credit scores between 500 to 579 are acceptable if you're able to make a larger down payment. Lenders may require a higher minimum score, but the FHA does work with scores as low as 500 or even no credit established at all. The down payment amounts are subject to your credit score history. However, it's important to note that due to the pandemic and recession, many FHA-lenders have raised their minimum credit requirements to a credit score of 620, so it's good to check with each lender. The FHA also likes to see a credit history of at least two lines of credit.

Low down payments are one of the FHA's main benefits, though bear in mind that if your credit score is below 580, you'll need to put down 10% of the purchase price. And even if you can get the 3.5% down payment, closing costs can add to that, so it's smart to save up to 6% of the purchase price to cover those, which include the 1.75% mortgage insurance premium. This premium can be lowered to 1.25% by taking an FHA-approved credit counseling program before closing. As mentioned, gift funds can be used for the down payment as long as you provide a letter with the donor's contact information, their relationship to you, the gift amount, and stating that repayment is not expected.

The main factor to qualify for an FHA loan is whether or not you can afford to make the payments. Two key areas are looked at to determine this. The mortgage payment cannot exceed 35% of your income before taxes, and your debt-to-income ratio must not be more than 48% of your income. This includes debts that you're not currently paying. If your debt is in deferred student loans, an FHA loan underwriter will include one percent of the loan's total as your monthly payment. For other types of loans that you aren't currently paying, the underwriter will use 5% of the loan's total.

FHA loans apply to a variety of property types, such as a house, condo, manufactured home, or multi-family property. However, there are minimum property requirements to be eligible. The FHA requires an appraisal that's separate from a home inspection. This appraisal is different since it only focuses on ensuring that the home meets basic safety and liveable standards and is a good investment. For FHA renovation loans, there will be two appraisals. One before the work is done to determine the "as is" condition, and one after the work as an "after improved" appraisal to reestimate the value of the home.

The application process for an FHA loan is straightforward and will require personal and financial documents. The applicant will need to have a Social Security number, proof of United States citizenship or legal permanent residency, eligibility to work in the United States, and bank statements for a minimum of 30 days, including proof of any deposits made. If you're unable to obtain some documents such as credit reports, tax returns, or employment records, the lender may be able to retrieve them for you. There are special circumstances for students or those without credit history that will require additional paperwork.

FHA loans are a terrific option for someone with little cash to hand, low income, and a credit score that could use polishing. They aren't as restrictive as the USDA and can be convenient if you've used crowdfunding to save up your down payment. Don't let the mortgage insurance premiums scare you away from them. If you're able to pay more than 10% of the down payment, you'll only need to worry about the mortgage insurance for 11 years. It can be a good incentive to save up between 6 to 10% due to this, but knowing you're still eligible if you can't is a comfort.

Another key point is that there is more than one type of FHA loan in which to choose. Each loan type has a specific focus and can help target your needs.

Types of FHA Loans

Understanding the specific types of FHA loans can be beneficial in the long term to ensure you're applying for a loan that meets the needs of your situation. Not only will we cover these types, but we'll also weigh the pros and cons of an FHA loan and key factors to consider when deciding. Even if you're already sold by this point!

The most standard type of FHA loan is the Fixed Rate FHA loan. These are the loans we've mainly discussed and are the ones with 15 to 30-year fixed mortgage terms. This type is handled similarly to a traditional mortgage, only with a low down payment advantage and low mortgage interest rates. Though lower credit scores are acceptable, it is common these days for lenders to ask for improved credit scores if your score is below 580. This type of loan covers most residences, which helps make finding a property easier. This includes condos, townhomes, manufactured and mobile homes, and both single-family and multi-family properties. However, multi-family residences can only be up to four units. The other factor to remember with this type of loan is that mortgage insurance premiums will be added to the loan amount as both upfront and annual costs.

If you're unhappy with the current rate for a fixed-rate loan, the Adjustable Rate FHA loan may be an alternative. These loans come with an interest rate that adjusts over the life of the loan, and they generally increase. There are three different term options to consider with this type: one and three-year adjustable-rate mortgages, five-year adjustable-rate mortgages, and seven to ten-year adjustable-rate mortgages. With the one and three-year option, rates can increase up to one point after the initial one to three-year fixed period, and the lifetime increase cannot exceed 5%. The same rule applies with five-year options, with rates increasing up to one point after five years with a lifetime increase capped at 5%. However, this option can also have a 2% increase per year after a five-year fixed period with a 6% lifetime increase limit. These terms are the same for a seven to ten-year option. Interest rates for these can increase 2% per year after a seven to ten-year fixed period with a lifetime increase capped at 6%. Most people who benefit from this type of loan are ones who plan to sell their home before their interest rate increases or people who received a pay raise and can afford a higher rate for their mortgage. Just be cautious with these types since rates are variable and unpredictable.

The next loan type is probably one you've heard mentioned on ads as reverse mortgages. This is called the FHA Reverse Mortgage and is a program used as a home equity conversion mortgage, or HECM. The HECM is a great option for older people who own their homes and need a way to increase their monthly income. It allows qualified homeowners to liquidate the equity on their homes to receive cash deposits either as fixed monthly payments or as a line of credit. However, since the HECM reduces the equity of your home, the FHA has set strict qualification requirements. To apply for this program, homeowners must be at least 62 years old, own the property outright or have a significant amount of equity, live in the residence the majority of the time, and be willing to complete a consumer education course that's held by a HUD-approved HECM professional. Other financial and property qualifications will also apply, and it's important to note that you'll still be responsible for fees and mortgage insurance premiums when closing. A HECM can be a useful option for many, but due to the reduction of equity in your home, considering other income methods first might be beneficial.

While searching for properties, you've come upon a house that you love, but it needs a lot of TLC. Fortunately, FHA loans cover fixer-uppers with their FHA 203(k) Improvement loan. This type of loan offers buyers the opportunity to purchase the fixer-upper home with additional financing for renovations and home repairs built into the mortgage. The guidelines for adding these financial add-ons allow for up to 110% financing of the appraised home value after the renovation work. Since this program was designed to include renovation projects, it's a great option for those wanting to purchase a fixer-upper and helps maintain and restore local neighborhoods as well. This loan can be extremely beneficial if you don't have much cash left after the down payment and your house requires renovations.

Similar to the FHA 203(k) option is the FHA Energy Efficient Mortgage, or EEM. This is another program that allows a financing add-on to include approved energy-efficient upgrades into the home loan. It works the same as the 203(k) but is aimed more for improvements that can lower utility bills, such as new insulation or installing solar panels. This loan is commonly used for updating windows and HVAC systems as well. The concept behind this loan is that by making the homes more energy-efficient, utility bills decrease, allowing the homeowner more money to make their mortgage payments. To qualify for this loan, an energy assessment will need to be performed on the house to prove that upgrades will be cost-effective.

For those who desire to pay off their mortgages early, the FHA loan known as Section 245(a) Graduated Payment Mortgage may be best for you. This loan is a fixed, typically 30-year mortgage that's also called the "growing equity mortgage." These types of mortgages schedule your monthly payments to graduated increases over the life of your loan. As the loan grows older, there will come a point where your equity will begin to increase more. If you have a job where you expect your income to increase, this could benefit you since it will allow you to pay off your mortgage early. The Graduated Payment Mortgage starts with low monthly payments that gradually increase over time to pay off the monthly principal. Paying off this much principal over time allows for shorter loan terms.

Though it's possible to buy a manufactured or mobile home with an FHA Mobile Home loan, it can be tricky finding a lender willing to do it. This is because mobile homes are often seen as personal properties and often have higher insurance rates, which makes them more of a risk to lenders. Due to this, the FHA has maximum loan amounts set for mobile homes. For only the home itself, the amount is $69,678. For only the lot, the amount is $23,226. And for both the home and lot together, the amount is $92,904. If you purchase only the home first, then the home can be placed on a leased lot, as long as the lease is for a minimum of three years. The maximum loan terms for mobile homes are also different and can range from 15 to 25 years, depending on the specifics of the home. For a single home or section for a single home with a lot, the term can be 20 years. If it's only a lot, the term will be 15 years. And if it is multi-sectioned for both home and lot, the term is 25 years.

Since many condo associations enforce rules on property sales, it can surprise people that FHA loans can cover condos. However, there are restrictions when considering an FHA Condo loan. The first is to check out the community for signs of stability, such as a high percentage of owner-occupied units, minimal non-residential square footage, few restrictions on buying and selling, and no rent-pooling agreements. To make your life easier, the FHA has a list of approved developments to choose from. However, because some associations allow their approval statuses to lapse, it's a good idea to confirm the current list before putting an offer in with an FHA loan.

Now it's time to weigh the pros and cons and make sure that there aren't any sneaky disadvantages you weren't aware of. We'll start with the drawbacks of an FHA loan, though fortunately there are only a few of them.

One of these is that there are limits to how much you can borrow for the loan. If for some reason the dream house you're longing for doesn't fall within the price bracket, you may be out of luck. This can be a deterrent for many, especially when accompanied by limited loan choices as well. A 15 or 30-year fixed loan may work for some, but occasionally there are instances when you may prefer an interest-only mortgage.

Another disadvantage to consider is the ongoing mortgage insurance premiums that you must pay. These payments added onto the loan balance for the long term can arguably make an FHA loan more expensive than a conventional loan, despite having lower mortgage rates. However, if your credit situation or lack of down payment makes an FHA the only viable option, then those mortgage insurance payments are worth it.

FHA loans can also cause hesitation in sellers, though this is only a possibility. Sellers like to know information about potential buyers and may be nervous with an FHA loan prospect, fearing delays in the selling process due to the extra requirements needed. This may pose a problem in a hot market where houses are selling fast.

Though we've covered many of the advantages of an FHA loan already, such as being approved with low credit and down payments can be gift-funded, there are a couple of other pros that FHA loans offer. These are the fact that sellers can cover up to 6% of the closing costs, whereas with a conventional loan, they could only cover up to 3%. And FHA loans allow a non-occupied co-borrower to co-sign for the loan if needed. This is especially helpful if you need a parent to help you obtain the loan.

When traditional resources are scarce or difficult to come by, an FHA loan is a wonderful alternative to get creative. By taking advantage of the government programs that exist to assist you, it can be easier to believe that your dream of homeownership is possible.

Chapter 5:

Are You a Veteran? Consider VA Loans

If you're one of the millions who have served in the American military, or your spouse has, then you have a unique option that traditional buyers can't take advantage of, especially if you lack the funds for a down payment. It's possible to qualify for a VA loan with little to zero down payment and barely any credit. Thousands of military personnel purchase homes through these loans every year. We'll explore what kind of loan it is, how to apply for it, and see if this alternative is the right choice for you.

The Veterans Administration estimates that 23 million people in the United States are eligible for the VA home loan. That's around one in every 13 people, and many are unaware that they could qualify. Anyone eligible should consider taking this opportunity, since VA loans have very low rates, usually lower than conventional loans, and they don't require a monthly mortgage insurance fee like USDA, FHA, or a conventional loan. This is another type of government-backed loan program which is insured by the U.S. Department of Veterans Affairs. The VA loan is guaranteed through private lenders, once again decreasing the risk and making lenders more flexible. The U.S. Department of Veterans Affairs also guarantees a percentage of each loan so that the borrower doesn't have to make a down payment or pay for private mortgage insurance. Depending on the private lender, it is also possible to have more forgiving credit score standards.

VA loans can be used more than once in your lifetime, but only for primary residences, not vacation homes or investment properties. You are allowed to build a home, remodel one, or update your home to make it more accessible for those with disabilities. Although it's commonly stated that VA loans have lower interest rates than conventional loans, this information is not always true. It's best to compare prices, or even look at the annual interest rates to get a better idea of how much the loan amount will truly cost. Right now, a 30-year conventional mortgage is slightly cheaper than a 30-year VA mortgage, but if you're able to find a specific lender who caters to veterans or active duty military service members, they may be able to offer you lower rates.

The process of a VA loan is simple. The Veterans Administration will provide paperwork for you to fill out to determine your eligibility. Once this is verified, you'll receive an entitlement, which is the dollar amount guaranteed for the loan. If this amount seems alarmingly small, don't worry. Some lenders are willing to loan up to four times the entitlement amount. Keep in mind that even though you won't have to make a down payment or pay for private mortgage insurance, VA loans require a one-time funding fee at closing, which is a percentage of the loan's total. This one-time fee is what helps keep the program running.

Now that we know how the process works, let's see the requirements necessary to make you eligible.

The Application Process

In general, to be eligible for a VA loan, you or your spouse are required to meet the basic service qualifications that are set by the U.S. Department of Veterans Affairs, have a valid Certificate of Eligibility, or COE, and also meet the private lender's credit and income requirements. Most people think that you must have served in the military for a long time to qualify, but the service requirements may be shorter than you think. The service requirements for regular service members is two years; for Reservists or National Guard, it's six years. If you've done active duty during wartime, it's 90 days, and if you've done active duty during peacetime, it's 181 days.

The first question you may have at the moment is what is a COE? The Certificate of Eligibility is an important part of the application process; however, you don't need to have it in hand when applying. A COE is proof of confirmation that you qualify for a VA loan through your military service and is provided to the lender. The reason it's not necessary to have it before applying is that most VA-lenders can access your COE through the VA's automated system. According to the VA, nearly all COE's are requested electronically, with about two-thirds of them being issued immediately. There are three ways you can obtain your COE, which are applying through a VA-lender, applying online through the VA's eBenefits portal, or applying by mail with the VA form 26-1880.

The documents required to obtain your COE are specific to the individual's service type. Often your documents for proof of service should be enough, such as a DD Form 214 for regular military and the NGB Forms 22 and 23 for National Guard and Reserves. However, different forms may be requested for certain types of service, so it's best to check to see which fits you. In addition to regular military service, if you're a veteran, current, or former Activated National Guard or Reserves, a DD Form 214 will suffice. If you're currently on active duty or Current National Guard or Reserves but never activated, then a Statement of Service will work. NGB Forms 22 and 23 are only suitable for Discharged National Guard who were never activated. However, Discharged Reserves that were never activated are separated by military branch and require specific forms for each. For Army Reserve, you will need a DARP Form FM 249-2E or ARPC Form 606-E. For those in the Navy Reserve, you will need form NRPC 1070-124. Members in the Air Force Reserve will need form AF 526, and Marine Corps Reserve will need either a NAVMC HQ509 or NAVMC 798. Lastly, Coast Guard Reserve members will need form CG 4174 or 4175.

Surviving spouses can often feel like they aren't eligible to receive the same benefits since they weren't active military, but this is not the case. In the past, surviving spouses could only be eligible for a VA loan if the spouse died on duty or due to a duty-related injury. However, at present, a spouse may apply if the veteran died of any cause, as long as they lived with a duty-related condition for a designated period by the VA and were eligible for compensation at the time of their death. It also applies to spouses of veterans with a Prisoner of War (POW) or Missing in Action (MIA) status. You can obtain your military spouse's COE, but it depends on whether or not you're receiving Dependency and Indemnity Compensation. If so, then you must fill out VA Form 26-1817 and get a copy of your spouse's veteran separation paperwork, such as a DD 214. However, if you're not receiving the Dependency and Indemnity Compensation benefit, you would fill out the VA Form 21P-534EZ and submit it to your state's VA Pension Management Center. Other documents that you'll need to provide are a copy of your marriage license, your spouse's veteran death certificate, or DD Form 1300, and your spouse's separation paperwork. All separation paperwork can be requested from the U.S. National Archives and Records Administration.

On average, when people think of the military, they only think of the main branches: Army, Navy, Air Force, and Marine Corps. Some may also think of the Coast Guard, but few people realize that there are seven uniformed branches in the military, and each one is eligible for VA home loan benefits. These branches are those just mentioned, plus Space Force, National Oceanic Atmospheric Administration, or NOAA, and Public Health Service, or USPHS. Members from certain other groups can also qualify for VA loans, such as West Point Academy Cadets, Air Force Academy, Coast Guard Academy, Midshipmen Naval Academy, and even next of kin for service members who are POW or MIA.

As with all government loans, there are eligibility requirements for the home as well. You may fall in love with a particular house, but it must meet the minimum requirements, called MPRs, set by the VA to be financed. During the loan process, a VA-certified appraiser will ensure that the house meets the requirements. They'll look to see if the home is safe, sound, sanitary, and has a solid foundation, with a stable roof and good overall structure. Basic necessities such as clean water, heat and power sources, and no health hazards are also confirmed. The home must also have access year-round to a well-maintained road and have specifically designated areas for cooking, living, and sleeping. If the home has pests, mold, rot, or broken windows, it will not pass. Depending on the property, there may be additional requirements, so it's best to check with your real estate agent before falling too head over heels.

After reading the minimum service requirements, you may still be in doubt as to whether your specific situation is eligible.

There are certain factors where you may still be qualified if you were discharged for one of the following reasons: personal hardship, government convenience, reduction in force, certain medical conditions, and a disability caused by service.

You may be ready by now to eagerly learn the application process to get started. However, before we set off on the steps to take, it's important to know that there are three types of VA loans to choose from so that you don't apply for the wrong one. The first type is the traditional VA Purchase Loan, where qualified members can purchase new or existing homes with zero down payment. These loans can be used for a variety of properties, such as single-family homes, condos, manufactured homes, new construction, and even multi-unit properties. However, policies and guidelines can be different with each private lender regarding purchase loans, so be sure to check.

The other two types of VA loans are refinancing options. The first is the VA Interest Rate Reduction Refinance Loan or known as the VA IRRRL. This is the most common choice for veteran homeowners looking to refinance. They're also called VA Streamlines since they're low-cost and simple due to cases that don't need credit underwriting, income verification, or even an appraisal. Of course, since this is a refinancing loan, qualified borrowers must already have a VA loan and are using it to get a new rate that's smaller than your current one, and have a time limit on how long it takes to gain back the costs and fees.

The second refinancing option is the VA Cash-Out Refinance loan. This allows qualified homeowners to cash out their equity by refinancing their mortgage and can be used for those with or without current VA loans. Using this loan, you can typically refinance up to 90% of your home's value. Private lenders will have varying guidelines and loan-to-value requirements. And since homeowners are not required to take out the cash from their equity, it allows non-VA mortgages to simply do a basic refinance for terms and rates.

Now it's time to begin your VA loan process! There are typically six steps to the application process, but when followed in order, it's fairly simple. The first step is to find a VA-approved lender. This is not as easy as heading over to your local bank. Only lenders who are approved by the U.S. Department of Veterans Affairs can finance VA mortgages. Also, most lenders only focus on conventional loans and may only process a few VA loans per year. These lenders won't be able to help you navigate through the process as easily as a lender who specializes in VA loans will. Using a lender with extensive knowledge about VA loans will help streamline the process.

Now that you have found a lender, it's time to obtain your COE, which the lender can help you with; or you can find it on the VA's eBenefits portal as we discussed earlier. The next step after this is optional, though recommended, and that is to get pre-qualified. Becoming pre-qualified can help save you time and some surprises later on down the line and can give you a stronger edge when looking for a house. When markets are fast, being pre-qualified is important so that sellers see you as serious buyers. To prequalify for your loan, you'll discuss your income, credit history, employment, marital status, and other factors that the VA lender will deem necessary. This step can also show you any red flags, such as debt-to-income ratio or credit issues that would need to improve before being approved. And though having a prequalification letter helps with house hunting, it doesn't guarantee loan approval, which will be done later after the lender has verified your information and the loan has been approved by underwriting once all documents are received.

Now it's time for the fun step, and that's the house hunt and signing the purchase agreement. Everyone enjoys this step because they get to shop for homes. A useful tip is to use a real estate agent who specializes in VA loans, the same as you did with your lender. The reason for this is because the VA allows the seller to pay certain fees and costs if agreed by you and the seller, and an agent knowledgeable with the VA process will know this and help with negotiations.

Once the purchase agreement has been signed, you give it to your lender, who will then order the appraisal. The appraisal is done by a VA-certified professional, who will not only follow the MPR checklist but also make sure that the home corresponds to the value placed on it. Though appraisals are infamous for taking a long time, the VA only gives the appraiser 10 days from the order to completion, aside from special circumstances. While waiting for the appraisal, you'll be giving your lender final documents to prove you can pay for the loan. Once the appraisal is finished, and the lender qualifies your loan, the underwriter will approve it.

All you have to do now is sign the loan agreement, provide proof of homeowners insurance, and pay closing costs if required. At this point, the keys are handed to you, and you can now move into your new home.

Benefits and Drawbacks

Veteran and currently active military service members have been enjoying the benefits of VA loans since before the end of World War II. After the Great Recession, the numbers of VA loans rose even higher, thanks to historically low rates and tougher lending requirements. The significant financial benefits that the VA loans offer have helped millions become homeowners who otherwise would not have qualified.

The biggest and most famous benefit is that you can purchase a home that's within your county's loan limit with zero down payment. When faced with 10% down payments for conventional loans and 3.5% for even an FHA loan, this is a significant draw for veterans, who would have had to save for years to come up with that kind of money.

The second-largest benefit is the fact that buyers don't have to pay for private mortgage insurance. This is arguably a bigger attraction than zero down payment, since like with FHA loans, private mortgage insurance can follow you for the life of the loan. Even conventional loans will require private mortgage insurance if you can't put down 20% of the purchase price. But no matter whether you put down zero or 10% on the home, VA loans will not require private mortgage insurance. They only require the one-time funding fee that goes to the Department of Veterans Affairs to keep the program running. And this is even exempt if you have a service-connected disability.

Another pro is that you don't need an excellent credit score to qualify for a VA loan. Though you will still need a minimum score of 620. However, VA loans will allow for higher debt-to-income ratios, with lenders ideally wanting no more than 41% of your monthly income spent on debt, but can allow up to 55%, depending on your credit score and income level. Having that flexibility helps maximize your purchasing power.

VA loans even protect you at closing by placing limits on what fees you will have to pay when it's time to close. This can save you lots of money in the end. Buyers can ask the seller to pay for all loan-related costs and up to 4% of the purchase price to cover taxes and insurance. Along with this, there are no penalties for paying your loan off early, like there are with conventional or FHA.

And though these words send a shiver of fear down any homeowner's spine, VA loans provide forgiveness with foreclosure and bankruptcy. Contrary to belief, these financial horrors don't prevent your chances of qualifying for a VA loan. If you've suffered from these situations in the past, don't give up hope. It's possible to qualify for a VA loan only two years after a foreclosure, short sale, or bankruptcy. There are even some cases where you can be eligible only one year after filing a Chapter 13 bankruptcy. Even if you have previously lost a VA-loan mortgage to foreclosure, you can still be eligible to apply for another.

Despite singing its praises, we have to admit that the VA loan does have its disadvantages. The first one being the most obvious, which is that it's not for everyone. The program is built in a way where the VA loan is a benefit you must earn by providing military service, which sets it apart from all other loan types.

And though it seems a fair trade for private mortgage insurance, the VA loan does have a mandatory funding fee to keep the program running. However, you can finance it into the loan if necessary. But if you reuse your VA loan benefit, the funding fee will be higher and increases with each use. However, you can lower the fee if you're able to pay a down payment.

It can also be limiting that the VA loan can only be used for a primary residence and is where the owner will live full time. You may also find that not all real estate agents are familiar with VA loans, which can be a setback when working through the buying process. They may show you properties that don't meet the VA's appraisal requirements or guidelines, and that can be a frustrating waste of time. Relative to this issue is that not all sellers are open to VA loan offers due to many years of misconceptions and myths surrounding this exclusive type of loan.

Over the years, there have been a variety of tales surrounding the VA loan, mostly because the majority of the general public didn't have access to it. However, even those who qualify can often be misguided by false information. Here is a list of ten facts about VA loans that are not commonly known.

They're reusable, and in more ways than one. A VA loan is not simply a one-time benefit. It can be used again if you wish to sell your current home and pay off the loan after the sale. Once the loan is paid off, your entitlement is fully restored, and you can purchase another home. The other way it's reusable is if you've paid off the loan but still live in the home. You're allowed a one-time restoration of your entitlement, and this applies even if you refinanced the VA mortgage with a non-VA loan.

Only certain types of homes can be purchased with a VA loan. If your dream is to buy a working farm, a business, or a fixer-upper, then a VA loan won't suit you. These loans are designed for homes in move-in condition and are limited to single-family, condo, multi-unit, and manufactured residences.

The home must be a primary residence, although multi-units are allowed as long as you live in one of the units. Then you can rent out the other units if desired. So if you're looking for a vacation home, you're out of luck.

You won't be disqualified if you have a past foreclosure or bankruptcy. Each lender will have its guidelines for this, but since the VA does not require a minimum credit score, it allows the lenders some flexibility. And the VA considers your credit fully restored after two years of clean credit history following a foreclosure or bankruptcy. The only exception is if the foreclosure was with a VA loan, in which that loan would have to be paid off to be fully eligible once more.

There's also no limit to how much you can borrow if you have a full entitlement. Qualified veterans can borrow as much as the lender is willing to allow. And no matter what the loan limit is, a down payment will not be required. For those without full entitlements, the VA and lenders use county-level limits to determine what kind of down payment might be needed, but if you have a fully entitled VA loan, this doesn't apply to you.

They're not issued by the VA. Though Veterans Affairs will guarantee the loan, only private lenders can finance them.

The government guarantees the loan, but only up to a quarter of the loan amount. However, this guarantee gives lenders confidence to work with military members who qualify and secure them at great rates.

If you didn't know it before, you know it now. VA loans don't have mortgage insurance. The VA's guarantee eliminates the need for mortgage insurance or any mortgage insurance premiums, which is a helpful way to save money every month. This also allows you to purchase a more expensive home since this payment isn't being deducted from your monthly income.

It does surprise people that a VA loan comes with a mandatory funding fee. Most people are aware of the zero-down payment and focus on that. But the funding fee is important and can almost be considered a way to give a helping hand to the other service members looking for homes since this fee keeps the program running.

Last but not least, VA loans don't have a prepayment penalty. If you come across a lump sum, you can pay off your loan at any time. Or simply make extra payments when you want, which can save you money on interest. You're even allowed to structure your payments to have automatic deductions taken every month.

So don't believe the misinformation floating around. VA loans may not be for everyone, but for those who can benefit from them, they can be a welcome relief.

Chapter 6:

Save Up!

Owning a home is the cornerstone to building wealth and the quintessential American dream. We've discussed many options with government loans, but if none of those appeals or apply to you, then don't give up hope on the traditional method quite yet. Though saving for a down payment the old-fashioned way may seem like a herculean effort, it is achievable. Consistently putting money aside feels slow and a lot like when we were kids stashing every coin we could get into our piggy banks. And though it didn't cost nearly as much to buy that toy we wanted as it does to buy a house, the principle of saving is the same.

The best place to start when deciding to save is to consider where you are in life and what you have. Making a checklist of your place in life can be emotionally beneficial, since it places you in the success mindset. Do I have a stable job? Yes. Do I have enough income at the end of the month to put aside? Yes. All of these small questions add up to a large answer when you're beginning down a daunting road.

These initial questions are a good place to set the foundation for a plan, but many other specific tips can be used to save for a down payment. Saving for a down payment is a little different than general savings. You don't want to simply start storing away however much cash you have without a plan. In the long run, you'll have a lot of money saved but no proper way to execute the strategy for buying a house. Saving for a down payment needs to be directed towards a goal, not storing coins in our piggy banks and waiting for the right amount to add up. Learning these ten tips will help you focus on the right areas to think of and clarify your target.

The first step is most likely one that you do already because it's what most people do while they're dreaming of owning a home. Researching home prices in your area by going online and browsing through home sales websites. This is not only fun but educational since it can show us what the realistic price of our dream home is and how expensive the area where we live is. Average prices per square foot vary greatly depending on your location. If you want to live in San Diego, California, but are currently living in Little Rock, Arkansas, your mental image of house prices is going to be worlds apart. So starting with a game plan on where you're looking will help, whether that's staying where you are or finding that you might have to move to afford a new home.

Now that you know how much your dream house will set you back, you can figure out how much you need to save. Saving blindly is the best way to save poorly. Having a set amount as a goal increases your odds of being successfully able to save that amount. It helps to meet with a lender to determine how much mortgage you could qualify for with your yearly income. In general, your house payment should not exceed 28% of your monthly income. And keep in mind that this amount will also need to cover the mortgage principal and interest, real estate taxes, private mortgage insurance, homeowners insurance, and even HOA fees, if applicable. You can avoid paying the private mortgage insurance by putting 20% down on the house's total cost, but most first-time homebuyers simply can't come up with that much money by the time they want to buy. So you have to weigh how much more you can afford to pay each month versus how likely it is you'll be able to save up 20% of a house's purchase price. This percentage amount is the ideal down payment since it gives you the best deals and lower rates.

However, if you can't achieve 20%, simply consider what the house's price would need to be to account for a higher interest rate and private mortgage insurance. The mortgage lender can help you calculate all of the costs and percentages you'll need to know to determine how much your down payment will likely need to be.

Unfortunately, the down payment is only one part of saving for a house. Your savings are also going to be hit by the other upfront costs associated with purchasing a home, such as appraisal fees, the home inspection, property taxes, and any other hidden fees that may occur during the process, depending on the home and type of mortgage loan. To help get a mental idea of what this looks like, the average closing costs in 2020 were $6,087, including taxes, and $3,470 without taxes. So once you know how much your down payment needs to be, add another six or seven thousand to account for closing costs and upfront fees.

The next step is to figure out your timeline and settle on it. When do you want to buy it? Deciding this will help determine how much money you can set aside each month. Oftentimes, your timeline is dictated by your budget. If your ideal plan is to purchase a home within two years, but you've figured out that you'll need to set aside 50% of your monthly income to save up in time, then you know it won't work. Knowing how much extra you have each month will help determine your timeframe. However, if you're an overachiever and will pull extra hours to do it, then simply dividing your down payment into two years will be fine. Just keep in mind that the shorter your timeframe, the higher your monthly savings will need to be.

There are creative ways to put that extra cash in your monthly budget to shorten the time frame, such as having a second job, paying off debt, or cutting back on luxury expenses. Cutting back on costs can be a quick way to put more money in your pocket and make more room in your budget for adding on a house payment. Saving for a down payment requires saving thousands of dollars per year. That kind of change in your budget is going to demand an alternative lifestyle. So instead of keeping with a Friday night pizza tradition, eat at home and store away that amount instead.

Now that we're storing away money, let's make sure we're putting it not only in a place we won't touch but also in a place that will be the most advantageous. Normal savings and checking accounts don't provide high interest, so experts suggest the best type of account to hold your savings are high-yield savings accounts or money market accounts. The higher interest rates these types of accounts provide will help grow your money faster. Even having this account at a separate bank can help prevent you from touching it. If your time frame is longer than five years, another option is to put the savings in a high-yield CD. Though you wouldn't be able to access it for a certain period, it'll be safe from an investment market and possibly even grow more interest than in a savings account.

Another tip is to fix this savings goal into your budget. Once you know how much you need and your timeline, you can decide whether this will be more achievable with a monthly or annual savings budget. Some people even budget by deducting a certain amount out of each paycheck. Or you can do a combination; for example, you know that every annual tax return will go into savings. So subtract that amount from the yearly total and then divide the remainder into monthly payments.

Also, don't underestimate any of the windfalls that come your way. Bank them! Windfalls are wonderful, sometimes unexpected, surprises that can boost our savings budgets. Take advantage of every annual tax return, monetary gift, bonus, or large commission check, or even when you decide to sell the boat. By regularly depositing yearly windfalls into your savings, you can end up decreasing your timeline by a couple of years.

One of the hardest parts of saving is the unexpected emergency that can occur. Having a savings strategy for your down payment goal is helpful and can make it possible, but it won't stop the unexpected from occurring, like your car breaking down or sudden medical expenses. Being flexible with your savings and having an emergency fund can help you prepare for the unexpected. Before you even begin to save for the down payment, make sure you have a well-funded emergency fund to help cover these sudden costs.

The last tip is one many don't think of since it's not directly related to saving, but improving your credit score can have a great effect on the total cost of your mortgage. The higher the credit score is, the lower the interest rate, which could potentially be a difference in thousands of dollars. So since saving for a down payment takes time anyway, take the opportunity to improve your credit score while waiting. These steps can include pulling your credit score to see what it is, paying down debt to lower your debt-to-credit ratio, resolving any disputes, and avoiding applying for new lines of credit as your timeline draws nearer.

These ten steps will improve the chances of saving success and make the process not seem so monumental. However, there is one step that needs a little more explanation since it can be imperative for your savings lifestyle, and that's to automate your savings.

Automate Your Savings for a Down Payment

Motivation and drive are always high at the beginning of our savings journey. We have our timeline, the amount we need to put aside each month, and now it's simply a matter of execution. However, this is when savings enters tricky territory. As time passes, and life happens around us, our priorities tend to shift, and often our savings are the first sacrifice. To prevent our savings from becoming scapegoats from the hazards of our life, a good rule of thumb is to create an automated savings plan. By doing this, we set ourselves up for success by implementing a tool that helps us from sabotaging ourselves.

An automated savings plan is a type of system for our personal savings in which a certain amount of funds are automatically deposited into our savings accounts at specified intervals. A typical example of this would be an automatic transfer from a person's bank account into a savings account every two weeks. Or that a certain amount of your paycheck is put into your savings account automatically. This can be convenient for someone who doesn't want or has a hard time remembering to manually deposit money every few weeks. It also helps to manage the budget and spending habits since you can't access the money.

Creating an automated savings plan is simple and straightforward. It's only linking a checking account to deposit into a savings account. However, figuring out how often and how much largely depends on your circumstances. Keep in mind that if you're automatically deducting from your paycheck, you need to schedule enough time for that paycheck to clear. When or even how often you make deductions doesn't matter as much as the consistency. It's easy to remain consistent when the automated savings is doing it for you.

It can also relieve a lot of mental stress in trying to remember not to touch a certain amount of money. Once it's taken from your paycheck or deducted from your account, you no longer have to think about it. It's like the age-old adage; out of sight, out of mind. This makes sticking to your budget much easier since you can't overspend. Instead of worrying over bills and expenses when you're paid and seeing how much you'll have leftover for savings, you'll simply need to think about the necessary expenditures with the comfort of knowing that even if you hit zero at the end, the savings amount has already been accounted for. Over time, you'll find that you don't even miss the money since your lifestyle has adapted to this new budget. And if an emergency happens, it'll be a surprising comfort to know you have a cushion to fall back on.

Online banking has made it very easy to set up automated savings plans. It's easy to open a savings account at your bank or even a different bank and link it to your checking account with a scheduled recurring deposit. If you have direct deposit from your employer, it becomes even easier. Simply ask your employer to have part of your paycheck deposited into the linked savings account and the remainder going into your checking.

This method sounds so simple you could think it's foolproof. And in many ways, it is, since it essentially is doing the work for you once it's set up. However, the most important part of this method is setting it up correctly. You'll want to be sure that you're utilizing your automated system to its full potential. You can do this by following five easy steps.

First, make sure you regularly monitor your budget to ensure that you still have that set amount for savings. When you created your automated savings plans, you might have had a certain amount of additional money to set aside. But since life changes, it's important to review your budget consistently to make sure you don't start putting aside more than you can afford.

Second, set clear goals for your automated savings plan, both for the short term and the long term. You know your long-term goal is a down payment, but maybe there's something else you want to save for as well that needs to happen before the house. You can always set up two separate accounts for each goal or simply add a little extra to your down payment savings to account for this short-term goal.

Third, as mentioned earlier, get the most for your money by choosing a high-yielding savings account. That high interest will work for you in the long run. When combining a high-interest savings account and automated system, your savings plan will be rock solid.

Fourth, be aware that many savings accounts have fees attached to them, so be careful that you choose one with the lowest fees possible. Having a high-interest savings account doesn't do you any good if all of the extra interest is going towards fees instead of your savings.

And fifth, be disciplined. Exercise caution when withdrawing from your savings account, and do it only when necessary. Saving money is a self-disciplined exercise, which is why it's so difficult. When your savings become a nice plump figure, it can be hard to resist the temptation to buy a high-priced item you've been wanting. One aspect that may help you, however, is the law under Federal Regulation D, which states that only six withdrawals per month are allowed. Any more than that will cause an excess withdrawal penalty charge.

Automated savings plans can be budget lifesavers. If you're too busy with life, let the automated savings plan system do it for you.

Seven Smart Investment Strategies

Having extra money can feel exhilarating, and the thrill of having it often overshadows any practical thinking about what we do with it. It could be that you inherited a large sum or received a sizable bonus. Whatever the reason you obtained this money, it's smart to know what to do with it so that it can not only be safe but grow. The main consideration is putting the savings somewhere that will grow interest, since if the savings isn't gaining interest, then it will be worth less over time due to inflation. Taking inflation into consideration, it's best to put your money into an investment plan where it can grow, you minimize the risk of losing it, and it adds value. Doing this can help you save your down payment faster. The best way to build savings is to allow it to grow slowly with little or no associated risk. There are a variety of different strategies to choose from where you can invest your savings and yield high results.

The most common place to save money is in a savings account, either from a bank or credit union. This is because the money is insured by the Federal Deposit Insurance Corporation or FDIC, but only up to certain limits. However, restrictions can apply to savings accounts, such as service fees, if you have gone over the allotted number of monthly transactions. In general, you can't withdraw money by writing checks with savings accounts, and in some cases, ATM use is also inaccessible. Traditionally, savings accounts also have low interest rates; however, due to online banking, there are now higher-yielding savings accounts.

As we briefly mentioned before, a good option for savings is a high-yield savings account. These are a type of savings accounts that are also protected by FDIC that earn a higher interest rate than the standard savings account. Interest rates can even go as high as one percent, as compared to a standard checking account interest rate which is merely 0.01%. However, it requires a larger initial deposit, and account access is limited by only allowing six withdrawals or transactions per month. High-yield savings accounts can be great options for building emergency funds or saving for vacations or home repairs. Many banks mainly offer these accounts to valued customers who already have a current account with them. They may even offer a sign-up bonus or bonus interest rate, but your minimum balance will need to be $5,000 to $10,000 to earn this rate.

If you're not a risk-taker and want the lowest risk option for a savings account, then consider a money market mutual fund. This is a type of mutual fund that only invests in low-risk securities, which is why it's one of the lowest risk funds available and provides a return that's similar to short-term interest rates. However, mutual funds are not insured by the FDIC but are regulated by the Securities and Exchange Commissions, or SEC. Many banks, brokerage firms, and mutual funds offer money market funds, but the interest rates are not guaranteed, so you want to take care to find one with a good historical performance.

Money Market Deposit Accounts can often be confused with mutual funds, but these types are more similar to high-yield savings accounts. They require a minimum upfront deposit and balance and have a limit on monthly transactions. Unlike money market mutual funds, they are insured by the FDIC, the same as the high-yield savings accounts. There are penalties with this option if you don't maintain your minimum balance or you surpass your monthly transaction allotment. They are a safe option if your bank is federally insured. Though their interest rates are typically lower than with certificates of deposits, you have easier access to your money since it isn't tied up for so long.

A certificate of deposit, or CD, is a completely different alternative to a savings account. With a CD, your savings are locked away for a set amount of time. If you make a withdrawal during this period, you will face a penalty. When interest rates are high, CDs can be wonderful since they have a fixed rate to protect you from falling interest rates. This can be a disadvantage, however, if interest rates are low, and since interest rates are variable, having your savings in a CD for the long term can end up not growing you as much money as if you had kept it in a savings account. This is why one strategy for CDs is called CD Laddering, where you open several CD accounts that mature at different times. This allows you the flexibility to take advantage of high interest rates as they happen.

If you know that you'll need at least five years to save for a down payment, then you need to think of an option that's more suitable for investments than savings. Investments can be scary since they generally have risks, but they do generate a higher return. A good option is a bond, which is a low-risk debt investment. These are issued by companies, states, municipalities, and governments to fund projects, and when you purchase a bond, you're lending money to one of them, making them now your bond issuer. In exchange, they pay for the interest on the life of the bond and return the bond's face value at maturity. Bonds are issued for a specific amount of time at fixed rates. All types of bonds carry a level of risk and penalties. You can receive a penalty for withdrawing early, for example, and commissions may be required. Depending on the bond, such as corporate, there can also be the additional risk of the company going bankrupt.

The safest place to invest your savings is treasury bills or notes since these are fully backed by the U.S. government and are federal, short-term debt obligations with one year of maturity or less. The longer they mature, the more interest you grow. They also have higher deposit insurance than money market accounts or CDs, which only offer deposit insurance up to $250,000. Treasury bills and notes are exempt from state and local taxes and sold at different maturity levels. There is a slight difference between notes and bills, however. Bills are sold at a discount and will only reach its full value when it matures. The difference between the purchase price and the face value is the interest it has grown. Treasury notes, however, are sold with varying degrees of maturity, which are two, three, five, seven, and ten years. They earn a fixed rate of interest every six months. If purchased at a discount, you can cash in notes for the full face value once they've reached maturity. Both treasury notes and bills must be purchased for a minimum of $100 and sold through brokers and investment banks.

For the daredevils out there who love taking risks, there are riskier options to invest your money. These options are for those who want to throw it all in and see what they can get out of it. There are three riskier options to choose from: stocks, gold, and real estate.

Stocks can potentially lead to high returns, but you'll need to be willing to ride the rollercoaster of the stock market. An S&P 500 index fund includes America's largest, most globally diversified companies across every industry and is a good place to start. It tends to be less risky than others and has returned about ten percent every year to investors.

During tough economic times, gold is a popular option. Opinions on gold vary greatly, where some think it's a safe place to settle your money, and others think it's too risky. This option is a personal one, but it can be lucrative.

The last riskiest option is real estate. Though you're still saving for a down payment, consider the investment value of climbing the real estate ladder once you're a homeowner. Real estate can be rewarding long-term investments by purchasing the home and renting it out, especially if you've been able to secure a low mortgage rate.

When saving for a down payment, it's important to remember to save smart and think long-term. How nice would it have been if that piggy bank as a kid automatically grew more money while it sat there? You want your money to work for you, and investing is the best strategy to accomplish this.

Chapter 7:

How About...Downsizing?

Do you ever feel like you're one of those hamsters running frantically on their hamster wheels? Many times we can be doing everything imaginable and still find that nothing has changed. It can feel like a vicious cycle and is one of the reasons people grow too frustrated and give up. If you're not getting anywhere, eventually you're going to get off the wheel and quit.

This is often because our lifestyles are spending the exact amount we're making, and unless we make a large change in our lives, this is going to continue. The most common culprit is what's taking the lion's share out of our salaries, and that is rent. This four-letter word of doom is the black hole in our bank accounts. You may argue that it's an unavoidable necessity, but getting rid of rent can make the difference between defeat or success in buying a home. Imagine if you could store away that rent money every month into savings. How much would you have after a year? The number that came up seems worth a lot of sacrifices.

It may seem challenging, but consider moving into a smaller place, or even back in with your parents or relatives, if possible. No one likes to feel as if they're taking a step back in life, but don't look at it that way. Think of it like making a large jump. When preparing to make a large leap, we step back to calculate the distance, the speed needed, and to gain momentum. This is what downsizing does for us. It allows us to prepare, calculate, and gain the momentum to move forward in our lives. If rent is weighing you down and preventing you from getting ahead, then it's time to cut the anchor and make a small sacrifice to downsize so you can prepare for a better life.

Remember, this move to downsize is temporary, and you can continue living a normal life while enjoying watching your savings grow faster than ever. There are many ways you can downsize rather than simply moving back in with your parents or cramming yourself into a studio apartment. Let's find which option you could live with the most.

How to Downsize Before You Upsize

When we look back into history, it can seem inconceivable that our distant relatives managed to survive in one-room cabins with a family of eight. But they did and never gave it much thought since that was simply the way life was. Over time, houses have grown in size, just as cities have grown in population. We made more money; we could afford to spread out a little more and be comfortable. There is nothing wrong with that; it was a natural progression of an advanced society. Unfortunately, since we've done nothing but expand over generations, many of us don't know how to downsize. When we want something, we find a way to fit it into our lives. But to upgrade your life, sometimes you have to sacrifice the luxuries and learn how to live a life more full of practical uses than cushy comforts. We're going to discuss the ways you can learn to downsize.

The first step is to do some self-evaluation and examine your expenses and priorities. This self-evaluation requires true honesty with yourself and can take some time to reflect on.

Your expenses are the perfect starting point since they can reveal what you're spending on and if it's something you truly need in your life. The first step in downsizing is to minimize unnecessary expenses and stop buying things simply because you can. Now sit back and think about your priorities. Make a list of your expenses and prioritize them to help see what you could live without. The pandemic has helped people in a way by forcing us to live without activities in our lives which we considered essential. You used to eat out three or four times per week. How much do you miss it? Have you learned to love cooking, or are you aching to get to the next restaurant? Consider these feelings and prioritize your expenses accordingly.

It's also important to understand what you can't live without when starting to downsize. If entertaining at home is important to you, then obviously a large living space and kitchen are essential. But perhaps you don't also need the large backyard or formal dining room. This is when you decide the areas you must have in your new home, and then anything after that is a bonus. Though you'll have to make sacrifices, be sure and make them in areas you know you won't miss. By thinking of the must-haves first, you can eliminate the chance of being stuck in a home you don't think is perfect.

Although you don't need to turn into a complete minimalist, decluttering your life is a critical step in the downsizing process. This is the time to clean out the attic and the garage. A good rule of thumb is that if you haven't thought about it or seen it in a year, then you don't need it. Take advantage of technology as well and see if perhaps there's a smaller, more streamlined alternative for certain items. Do you need 30 recipe books, or can you simply find a recipe blog or website online? Reevaluating ways to have stuff can help you declutter all the superfluous items you own.

A nice incentive to downsizing is that you can make a little extra money with a yard sale or donate to charity. Or even passing it on to someone who could use it and feel good that you helped someone out. It may even surprise you to find useful items you forgot you owned. Before buying something new, always check your hidden nooks and crannies to be sure you don't already own them.

Downsizing requires more than simply focusing on the physical items you own or the place you live. It also affects our lifestyles, especially our social lives. Most people have friends and hobbies that may be affected by our lifestyle changes. For example, you always meet your friend for lunch on Saturdays. Don't cancel on them, but perhaps rearrange the plan to meet at your house instead, which will save you money on eating out. Our social habits also have to be factored in our downsizing decision since they reflect our expenditures and our priorities.

You also need to make a plan once you've envisioned what you want your life to be after downsizing. Since changing a lifestyle is fairly involved, it's important to break it down into stages so that it can be more achievable. Every change requires a plan to execute it. If you've decided to embrace your inner chef instead of going out to eat, that's going to require some meal planning and a new schedule to make time for cooking. Setting small goals in stages allows you to downsize without getting too overwhelmed and is a way to prioritize your life. Choose a lifestyle change you can live most without, and start from there. Once done, move onto the next priority, and so forth. Little by little, you'll see that your life is downsizing.

It's also important to be very realistic with what you need. You may adore and worship shoes, but at the end of the day, you only have two feet to wear them at a time. So do you really need 20 pairs of shoes? Shoes take up loads of closet space, so by downsizing to perhaps three or four pairs, you can automatically create a smaller living space. Another chronic collection item that tends to build up in people's kitchens is mugs. It isn't possible to use 15 mugs at any given time unless you throw massive parties consistently. Choose your favorite six and declutter your cupboards.

The last step is to prepare for life's changing circumstances. This is by far the trickiest since we have to think about the unknown, but if you take the time to reflect on your life, it's easy to imagine the future, especially since we decide what we want our future to be. For example, if you're married and know that children are in your future, account for that when downsizing. It isn't realistic to think that a child may not happen while you're saving, even if it's not in the plan. So perhaps an extra bedroom isn't out of the realm of reality. You want to allow yourself some flexibility for circumstances that may surprise you. Saving for a house takes some time, and life still goes on. Downsizing can benefit your pocketbook and even your lifestyle in a way, but it needs to be able to adapt to any changes that may happen in the meantime.

All of these steps can help make downsizing attainable, and by doing them in stages, they are less overwhelming. If we were honestly looking at the items we own, we would realize that luxury and comfort have far overtaken life's necessities. Over generations, we've gotten so accustomed to getting what we want that we never take the time to think of what we need. They've become interconnected, and we would be amazed at how much we can live without. Downsizing has many benefits, but it's not easy. Many people struggle to do it, and for good reason. There are disadvantages to downsizing as well, and we will cover both. However, the most important part to remember is that downsizing doesn't mean sacrificing everything you enjoy or stopping your lifestyle completely. It simply means prioritizing what's important.

The Benefits and Disadvantages

Downsizing can be a harrowing and emotional journey filled with many moments of hard decisions. It can be easy to wonder why you're bothering during these times. It helps to keep in mind the multiple benefits that come with downsizing. Focusing on the positive aspects will help ease the burden of the challenge.

The first benefit is the most obvious, and that is saving money, not only on rent but on every frivolous item you may own. The larger your house is, the more inclined you are to fill the space, even with items you don't need. If an item is filling space more than fulfilling a function, then it's not necessary. By living in a smaller space, you can stop wasting money on surplus furniture, appliances, and electronics that you simply bought because they fit in the house.

Enjoying the benefits of smaller living allows you to appreciate that life holds more when you own less. This may sound like an oxymoron, but think about the added stress and upkeep large homes require. There's more to clean, furnish, and a higher cost to run. Unless you have a full staff maintaining your home, it can be a lot of stress to keep up with all of it. When you live in a smaller home and own fewer items to fill it with, you'll naturally start enjoying a more streamlined life that's free from the worry of outdoor upkeep and housework. As your daily chores decrease, you'll find your peace of mind increasing, and you have more time for luxury activities. This can be spending more time with your family, resting in that hammock more, and could even lead to you loving your home even more.

No one typically considers this, but when we live in a large house, the family is spread out and hardly notices one another. One of the benefits of a smaller home is a happier family. This can naturally occur by shifts in daily living where family members have to be next to each other more. Smaller homes force you to become organized and work together to create compromises over living arrangements, such as sharing closet space or doing homework at the same table. This may seem like a recipe for bickering, but families in small homes have agreed that their family bonds have tightened since moving into closer conditions.

Downsizing can even help the environment and make you proud to change your footprint from carbon to green. If you've lived in a large home, you know how expensive the energy costs were, such as heating, water, and electricity. By reducing the size of your home, all of these costs are reduced as well, which benefits not only your wallet but also the environment. Another way to reduce costs even further is by moving into a town where you can walk more, therefore lessening your fuel costs in driving.

Try to think of downsizing as opening a new chapter in your life. It can represent starting a new life and enjoying a new home. A different change of pace, environment, and even lifestyle can provide new experiences and opportunities. Since you have less home to maintain, you can have more time for traveling, picking up a new hobby, or even meeting new neighbors. This new chapter can be an exciting stage in your life while you prepare for the next stage.

Renovations or improvements to your home are also much easier when you're living in a smaller house. It may even be worth considering saving a down payment for a lower mortgage so that you have more money to buy new appliances, improve flooring, or any other home projects you would like to do with the house. This isn't to say you need to buy a fixer-upper when downsizing, but purchasing a smaller, less expensive home gives you more financial flexibility to play with the house more.

If living in smaller arrangements is new to you, you may enjoy the benefit of urban living that downsizing can provide if you choose to live in the city. It can be difficult living in a one-bedroom apartment in the middle of a suburban area filled with houses since you're constantly having to look at others living in larger homes. But if you surround yourself with neighbors living in the same conditions you are, a sense of community can be established. By watching others, you can learn to make the most out of your space by filling it with color, multifunctional furniture, wall art, plenty of light, and creative space methods.

Don't be fooled by thinking that downsizing means you're moving into a grungy living space. It can be easier to decorate a small home with quality pieces of furniture and decor than a larger one since you don't need to buy as much. You can still showcase a sense of style and creative decor in a small house or apartment. Size should not hinder you from showing off how functionally you can use your smaller space.

Now that you've decluttered all of the surpluses and kept only the essentials, you can see how much space you need. This is a great opportunity to get creative with organizational tricks and furniture uses. Built-in bookshelves, vertical organizers in closets, and dividing spaces into different sections can all be ways to make the most out of your area. Incorporating space-saving methods and creative techniques can help your home look efficient instead of cramped.

The main reason why downsizing is beneficial for those trying to save money is that it prevents you from overspending on products you don't need. If you can't fit it into your house, you're less likely to buy it. A smaller lifestyle will help keep you on budget while you save, and a lack of overspending will help keep your credit in the red as well. Simply cutting back on your lifestyle will make a significant difference in your finances and help saving become that much easier.

However, it's important to be aware of the disadvantages that might be waiting for you with downsizing as well. This option doesn't work for everyone, especially if moving in with relatives isn't an alternative for you. To make an educated decision on whether downsizing is right for you, we need to look at the negative viewpoints as well.

Moving anywhere costs money. Though the property may be smaller and less expensive to maintain, the cost of moving into it can be high. Since you're saving for a down payment, it would most likely be a rental property you would be moving to, which is good since it can show you what living in smaller spaces is like. However, there are costs attached to this, such as hiring a moving van, renter's insurance, and possibly even storage facility rentals if you kept more than could fit into the house. All of these expenses are before you move in and factor in costs such as new furniture or any repairs or maintenance.

Adjusting to a new home and new neighborhood can also be challenging, especially if you've lived in your previous one for a long time. Each home has different secrets to discover, so you'll have to learn all of the new nuances of your new home. You may also have to familiarize yourself with new neighbors, new places to shop, bank, and even eat.

A hard disadvantage to overcome is the loss of storage space. As much as it's nice to declutter and rid your life of unwanted items, the lack of space for the stuff you keep is difficult. A good way to think of it is that for every square foot less space, you have to get rid of items to accommodate for that loss of space. This means if you move from a 2,000 square foot home to a 1,000 square foot apartment, you have to get rid of enough items to account for that loss of space. Fortunately, many traditional items now have turned digital, so if you have multiple boxes of movies, books, and photo albums, all of these can be transferred onto digital devices to save space.

If you're social and like to entertain, downsizing can be a huge disadvantage since now you'll have less space for entertaining. This can be a critical setback for someone who's used to hosting all the family functions or friends' parties. Before downsizing, be sure and factor in your social life if you're used to entertaining. However, alternative arrangements are possible by renting a space to host the party instead or going away on family trips for the holidays.

We cannot underestimate the importance of the biggest disadvantage to downsizing, and that is the emotional impact it has on us. Making such a large transition in our lives can cause sadness, grief, stress, and even anxiety. Two emotional factors must be considered when downsizing, and those are mental obstacles and emotional barriers. Both of these can cause you to feel overwhelmed at the thought of making such a drastic change.

Mental obstacles happen in the very beginning when you're trying to cope with how to prioritize your beloved belongings. Not to mention the overwhelming task of going through all of it, especially if you have large amounts of storage in a large home. Another worry is if you don't have the physical help to move and wonder how you're going to pack everything and physically move it to the next home.

However, mental obstacles can be overcome with practical solutions, whereas emotional barriers are the hardest to cope with. When making such a large change and facing so many difficult decisions, it's understandable that downsizing can make people feel depressed, anxious, stressed, indecisive, sad, and overwhelmed. Homes are associated not only with comfort but years of memories. Leaving behind a place where you have mentally attached many happy times can be heartbreaking.

It may be tempting to let these mental and emotional obstacles make you procrastinate on making this decision, but there are coping methods you can use if you know it's the right choice. Instead of trying to manage the entire move on your own, ask for help from family and friends, both emotionally and physically. If they can't help you with the moving process itself, hire a professional moving company to take care of everything for you. They load everything into the truck, unload everything into the new home, and can even set up beds and place furniture in the correct rooms. Many of these companies will be willing to take all of the empty boxes as well once you've unpacked.

You should never allow yourself to be alone when downsizing if you're struggling with the emotional aspect of it. Downsizing is preparing for a new life and leaving behind one filled with memories. It's natural to feel emotional, but by focusing on the new growth and experiences ahead, you can work through the obstacles towards a better future.

Chapter 8:

You Could Also Make More Money

The journey to homeownership is lined with challenges and sacrifices. It's a journey that many people only want to make once, especially the first time. Finding extra funds to channel towards your down payment can sometimes feel like a magic trick, but there are several ways to earn extra cash these days. Cutting back expenses can only work so much before compromising your quality of life. And honestly, decreasing your budget doesn't give you the extra amount that earning more money can.

We're going to explore the different methods and available options in which you can begin earning more money to help your finances. Boundless opportunities are out there for people with all levels of experience, and in this digital age, the amount of online choices is vast. Obviously, the more experienced you are, the more money you'll earn, but even those beginning with the lower-earning jobs will build up revenue over time.

These methods of earning extra money can vary widely in the range of compensation and expertise. Consider the per-hour rates you will earn when looking at an option since you want to be sure that it's worth your time. So if you've already decreased your budget and cut back costs all you can, let's see how much more money you can earn!

Making Extra Cash

Though it can be a scary prospect that many avoid, attempting to change your job can be beneficial in the long term. However, this may not apply to you if you have a professional career and a high income. The way this works is if you have a special skill that a company wants. At this point, you have the most leverage since they want you but don't know if they can get you. When negotiating salaries, use this to your advantage to get the best salary possible. Changing jobs can also potentially set you up for future higher earnings since your starting pay will already be higher.

If you're already happy with the company you work with, you can do the next scariest task of asking for a raise. However, as we all know, this can be risky since the company is content with your current salary. You have to develop a strong argument that you deserve the raise.

Many people can't really change their job situations, so another method is freelancing. This is the next best way to be paid for your work since professional work always pays more than unskilled. Contacting professional colleagues or other personal connections can help you find opportunities, as well as connecting on LinkedIn. You can also post on marketplaces that are specific to your field. There are many freelancing websites in which you can search for opportunities, such as Elance-Odesk and Fiverr, though some freelancers do warn that these service providers can create fierce bottom-rate competition, so sometimes they are not lucrative.

You can also offer to coach other colleagues in your field. Create a website, or add a section if you have one already, describing what you'd offer as a coach. You can advertise these services on industry forums. It's a good idea to give new clients a discount or other incentive so that they're more likely to refer you.

Monetize your expertise by offering to tutor, whether for adults or students. There are established tutoring groups, like Kaplan, that specialize in SAT tutoring, or you could try freelancing your own tutoring services for a more specific subject you excel in and advertise your service to parents, schools, and community centers. If you want to only tutor adults, then create a website or list your services with adult tutoring companies.

Believe it or not, many offices still need temporary workers, so traditional temp agencies like Kelly Services still exist and list temporary work opportunities. You can also find temporary positions available on Indeed.com, which searches by location.

After work, if you have spare time in the evenings, you can offer to get paid to run errands. Signing up with companies like TaskRabbit or Zaarly is a great way to find those opportunities. You can also put notices up on community boards that you're available to do grocery runs or, if capable, be a handyman for those who need miscellaneous household tasks.

An option that can awaken the animal lover in all of us is being a dog walker. Ask friends, family, or neighbors if they want their dogs walked during the day, especially if you have a flexible work schedule. Many people dislike their dogs being home alone while they're at work and are more than happy to pay someone to spend quality time with their beloved canines. You can even post your services on dog walking websites.

Waiting tables or bartending can also be terrific methods for extra income and particularly lucrative in tips. You could even look into being a waiter for a catering company if that's more your style. Find a local company looking for cater waiters, or go to the website Waiters to Cater to search for opportunities.

Doing yard maintenance is a popular one since no one likes to mow lawns, rake leaves, or shovel snow. Offering these services to neighbors, friends, and family is not only good physical exercise but a good way to make some pocket money that can add up. You can also post notices on local community boards.

If you adore playing with little ones, offer babysitting as a side income job. You can use websites like SitterCity to post your services or ask friends, family, and neighbors if they need a babysitter or know families who need one.

Artistic skills can always be put to use for extra income, so if you have a photographer or musician inside you bursting to come out, then offer to use either service at weddings. If you have a portfolio site, list your services, or advertise at weddings or commercial events. You can also use website sources such as Thumbtack, Gigmasters, Gigsalad, WeddingWire, and Snapknot.

An easy one to opt for is to write software reviews, especially if you only have limited time and don't like advertising services. A website called SoftwareJudge.com offers a pay range from $1 to $50 for original reviews. The only stipulation with this is that you may need to try out different products to broaden your knowledge.

Another job you can do online is to get paid for doing online searches. Again this doesn't require any advertising and is something that can be done with limited time availability. If you add Qmee to your browser and click on the search results that it offers, you can earn some money. It isn't much, but click on enough results, and it can add up.

If you specialize in your field or have a specific area of expertise, many people could use your help. You can offer to teach online courses on websites such as Udemy or Skillshare. Teaching online can be flexible, part-time work, and a real benefit is no commute!

You can also put your good cooking skills to work if you happen to have any. When you entertain, and your guests are always commenting on how wonderful your food is, take the opportunity to put this skill to good use by getting paid to create memorable meals for clients through the website KitchenSurfing.

Shopping can be detrimental to saving, especially if you have a fondness for it, but it doesn't have to be. Why not shop to make extra money? You can do this by becoming a mystery shopper. You get hired to shop and report your experiences. However, be aware that there are many mystery shopping scams, so the safest way to find legitimate opportunities is to go through the Mystery Shopping Providers Association.

Not to kick you out on the streets, but if staying at a relative or friend's place temporarily is an option, you can make good extra income by renting out your home for short periods. You can even only rent out an extra room if available instead of the whole house. Visitors to areas are starting to stray from hotels and prefer to rent out homes through websites, such as Airbnb or VRBO.

Being an opinionated person can be lucrative as well if you participate in focus groups. These groups pay you to give your opinions on products and experiences. You can find opportunities on websites such as Focus Pointe Global, Inspired Opinions, Harris Poll Online, SwagBucks, MySurvey.com, Toluna, Opinion Outpost, iPoll, and Hiving.

Ever wonder if you could make money as a guinea pig? Well, in a manner of speaking, you can! Become a test subject when researchers run clinical trials. They need healthy subjects to use as a control group against the patients who have the illness. If this sounds intriguing, you can find more information from the National Institutes of Health and search for clinical trials at ClinicalTrials.gov. You would have to contact your local university for any psychological studies.

As you can see, earning an extra income has never been easier. Gone are the days of pounding the streets asking for odd jobs or placing flyers on telephone poles and shop windows. The digital age has opened up an online world full of creative ways for people to make a side income. If you can be open-minded, creative, and flexible enough to learn, the opportunities are out there waiting for you.

Passive Income

In addition to earning extra income through jobs on the side, another stream of revenue you can use to earn money is having a passive income. If you don't have the time for extra jobs on top of your full-time job, passive income can work perfectly since it doesn't require a lot of time. When done correctly, a passive income can be a lifeline to your savings. Passive income is when you earn money through any enterprise that requires little effort or maintenance on your part. In other words, this is money you can be earning while you sleep. Building multiple streams of passive income can help you prepare for any financial shocks in the future as well. It is a long-term choice and will require short-term tradeoffs, but if you commit to the resources, you can have a lucrative benefit for years.

However, don't misunderstand the word passive to think that you don't need to do anything and the money will keep rolling in. Eventually, this is the goal, but it does require time, money, and skills to nurture it in the beginning, often even needing an upfront investment to get it started. After some hard work and time, these income streams will gain momentum until they can maintain themselves, and that's when you can bring in consistent income without much effort on your part. The main point of passive income is to save you time while still increasing your funds. Oftentimes, setting it up can feel discouraging, since your effort is high and you're not earning money. But once the foundation is built, it's simply a matter of maintaining it while it makes money. So effort is minimal, and the rewards are great.

As good as this sounds, don't quit your day job once you have passive income. It's meant to supplement an income or help with retirement and save you time so you can enjoy doing more which you love. Investing in stocks is also not passive income because stock appreciation is not income.

There are steps to building a passive income since it's impossible to directly begin saving time and earning money. In the beginning, you're simply planting the seed to nurture it to grow. That can be as easy as starting a blog or investing $100 into a robo-advising platform. The first step is to start building a nest egg. Open a high-yield savings account and deposit $100 into it. That's passive income since now that money is going to build interest whether you do anything or not. The second step is to assess your skills, amount of time you have, money, and desired effort. Think about what you specialize in and research the different ways others with those skills have created income streams. Time is our most limited resource and can be difficult to manipulate. Though learning how to create passive income takes time, especially if you have to learn a new skill, keep in mind it's temporary, and this will change in the long term. You also want to consider the amount of effort you want to put in.

If you're busy with family, friends, and work, then investing might be a better passive income method for you.

The final step is to come up with some ideas and choose those you like best. Let's explore some of the options out there, keeping in mind the different levels of effort required, the time needed, and the upfront investment.

Investing in real estate has been a popular method of passive income for years. It requires the upfront cost of buying the house and maintaining it before renting it out and making passive income from your tenants. However, if you don't have the funds to buy a house or the time to be a landlord, you can still invest in real estate through Real Estate Investment Trusts. REITs own and manage income-producing properties, then distribute the profits to investors. In the past, this used to be expensive, and you had to be an accredited investor, but the company Fundrise changed those rules completely. They offer a variety of options, and the minimum investment is $500.

A time-tested passive income is stock market investing, but if you don't know much about it or don't enjoy picking out dividend stocks, that's all right since it won't prevent you from still being able to passively invest in stocks. You do this through a robo-advisor, which is a robotic financial advisor. This system is set up with an algorithm that manages your investments. All you have to do is answer a few questions, set up your account, and the robo-advisor takes it from there. A trustworthy robo-advisor is Betterment, which allows you to set your risk level, and has much lower fees than if you chose a human account manager. Betterment will also help reduce taxes on your investment, and they give you financial advice. They're also one of the few robo-advisors that let you talk to a real person if you desire.

Peer-to-peer lending is another method of passive income or P2P lending. This is when you lend money to individuals or a business, and they pay you back, with interest. You do this through a company called Lending Club. The borrower needs a loan for $5,000. So they create an account with Lending Club, and depending on their credit history and income, they're given an interest rate on the loan. You also create an account with Lending Club and buy the debt. The borrower then makes monthly payments to Lending Club, and you earn the interest and principal in your Lending Club investment account. While Lending Club deals primarily with personal loans, a company like Worthy deals with business loans, but each company processes the same way. The expected return is 5%, and though that may not sound like much, 5% is more than national bank interest rates.

You may have heard about starting a blog being a great way to earn money, but you weren't sure how that worked. Starting a blog is a passive income method and uses affiliate marketing to earn money. Affiliate marketing is when you partner with a company to receive a commission on the product. This works best if you have a blog or website to post an ad for that company. It does take a long time for the money to become passive since you have to spend time consistently using your blog. The more creative posts you make, the higher traffic you'll attract, and the higher odds for people to see your marketing ads. The easy part about using this method is that it requires almost no upfront cost. Blogs can be started for as little as a penny and cost only a couple of dollars per month.

Network marketing is another method, though it can have higher upfront costs and does require maximum effort to get started. Despite this, these companies you can partner with are becoming more popular due to people being able to be their own boss, set their own schedule, and have flexibility. Networking marketing is a business model where private contractors (you) buy into a company. When you sell their products, you earn a commission. There are a variety of ways to make money with the company, such as building a team under you to earn a percentage of their commissions and recruiting others to join.

Self-publishing is becoming incredibly popular and is one of the mainstream ways of publishing these days. If you have the skills or desire to write an ebook, getting it published has never been easier. Simply write it, have it edited, create a cover, and then upload it to numerous publishing websites, like Amazon Kindle Direct Publishing. However, writing an ebook does require a lot of upfront marketing, which means time, effort, and expense. But once it's gaining sales, it can be an easy passive income stream.

If you thought taking photos was only for capturing memories, think again. Depending on how much you enjoy it and your skill level, you can sell stock photos. Websites, blogs, and even magazines buy their photos from stock photo websites, such as Adobe Stock, Shutterstock, Alamy, or DepositPhotos. You can submit your photos to these websites and receive a commission whenever someone purchases them.

Licensing music is another way to put your creative talent to good use. If you love making music but have never desired to be on stage, then licensing your music could be a good option. It means that people pay you for the rights to your music so they can use it in a project. Often, music is licensed for YouTube, podcasts, and even commercials. Now that people are creating more videos and podcasts than ever, music is in even higher demand.

By this time, almost everyone owns and uses a smartphone and usually has loads of apps. You can make a tidy profit by creating and building an app as a way to share your skills or services. Hiring a programmer to build the app can get expensive, but if you're open to learning, you could build one or even barter their services. Once the app is created, you can sell it on the App store to create a passive income stream. This method can also go hand-in-hand with selling products if you're crafty or artistic. Websites like Etsy help you build a storefront and sell unique products online.

While building a passive income stream can take time, money, and patience, it's well worth the effort for a lifetime of effortless income. It doesn't matter if you have millions of dollars to invest or zero. If you have the time and the creativity to get it started, it can work for you. Assess your situation, your financial capabilities, and see which method sounds the most promising.

Conclusion

Hopefully, this has been an exhilarating journey learning about the different paths to homeownership. We're back at your previous home staring at that For Sale sign, only now, you should have a sense of hope and purpose more than one of despair. As you have learned, there are too many programs, loans, and methods available for anyone to feel like owning a home is out of reach. And if someone tells you differently, you have the knowledge now to correct them.

A lot of this knowledge can take time to understand and implement. Especially when deciding which method will work best for you. Perhaps crowdfunding sounded the most appealing, since joining a platform is relatively simple, and it widens your opportunities for people to contribute. After all, crowdfunding has worked for people since the early 18th century; there's no reason it can't work for you. It's also a nice way of sparing your family and friends from feeling pressured to donate towards your cause.

You should also know your plan to improve or build your credit and do more research into getting lines of credit. This is the best place to start since no matter which option you choose, having trustworthy credit will always benefit you. The variety you have to choose for lines of credit is also helpful, be it from home equity, personal, or business. There's a line of credit for anyone, so it's simply a matter of knowing which one applies to you.

It's amazing to know how many different types of loans there are and how many government programs, such as the USDA,

FHA, and VA loans. These loans are great examples of why anyone can own a home, regardless of their position, if they do their research and educate themselves. Be proud that you can say you're one of those people. You have stepped outside your comfort zone and opened your eyes to the possibilities out there. In that simple step, you have increased your chances of success. Perhaps the USDA loan even made you consider a rural home that you wouldn't have otherwise thought about. Or the FHA loan made you realize that it isn't necessary to have a 20% down payment, but that you could even have as little as 3.5%. And certainly, if you're a military service member, it is imperative that you know about the VA loan so that all your years of service don't go unrewarded.

Even if none of the loans or programs seemed to be a good option, now you know how to save, which is a skill many don't have. Saving is incredibly challenging and can be tricky to incorporate into your life. With this knowledge, you can utilize these savings tips to their full potential. This can be especially exhilarated if you consider downsizing and minimize your expenses with that method. Though downsizing is a decision that can be heavy with emotion or doubt, it has long-term benefits that make it worth it. Often, the hardest decisions are usually the ones that are for the best, especially when needing to make large life changes. Stepping out of the rental rut and onto the road to being a homeowner is a monumental life change, but only for the better. The immense joy your own home will give you will outweigh the grief of downsizing.

You are also now filled with the knowledge of how to make more money. Side incomes and passive incomes can be surprisingly lucrative when you put in the effort. Not only are they beneficial to your bank account, but these are wonderful ways to boost self-confidence, since many times you learn new skills in the process. Perhaps even find a new hobby when trying something new, such as photography. Knowing that there are legitimate ways to earn more money can inspire hope that your day job doesn't have to be your only source of income. Most side incomes or creating passive incomes end up being more enjoyable anyway.

So say goodbye to that For Sale sign in front of your once beloved home. Thank it for the memories, and walk away. You're heading somewhere better now, armed with the tools needed to become a homeowner.

If you enjoyed this book, please leave a review on Amazon.

References

10 Things to Know About VA Home Loans - NewHomeSource. (n.d.). Www.newhomesource.com. Retrieved July 5, 2021, from https://www.newhomesource.com/learn/va-home-loan/

10 Things to Know About VA Loan Eligibility. (2021, February 4). Military.com. https://www.military.com/money/va-loans/va-loan-eligibility-10-things-to-know.html

Alexander, F. (2020, August 13). *How to Save for a House Down Payment*. Clever Girl Finance. https://www.clevergirlfinance.com/blog/how-to-save-for-a-house-down-payment/

Azzoli, D. (2019, August 27). *Different Types of Lines of Credit*. MoneyKey. https://www.moneykey.com/articles/different-types-of-lines-of-credit/

Bank, F. R. (2020, August 25). *5 Tips for Finding the Best Personal Line of Credit*. First Republic Bank. https://www.firstrepublic.com/personal-line-of-credit/5-tips-for-finding-the-best-personal-line-of-credit

Bank, F. R. (2020, November 14). *Types of Lines of Credit: What's the Difference?* First Republic Bank. https://www.firstrepublic.com/personal-line-of-credit/types-of-lines-of-credit

Birk, C. (n.d.). *6 Unbeatable Benefits of VA Loans*. Military.com. Retrieved July 5, 2021, from https://www.military.com/money/va-loans/6-unbeatable-benefits-of-va-loans.html

Birk, C. (2019, September 20). *VA Mortgage Pros and Cons - Weighing the Benefits of the VA Loan*. Veterans United Network. https://www.veteransunited.com/valoans/va-loan-pros-and-cons/

Birk, C. (2020, October 6). *How VA Loans Work: What Most Borrowers Don't Know About VA Loans*. Veterans United Network. https://www.veteransunited.com/valoans/10-things-many-borrowers-dont-know-about-va-loans/

Breeding, B. (2018, October 1). *Overcoming the Mental Obstacles & Emotional Barriers of Downsizing*. MyLifeSite. https://www.mylifesite.net/blog/post/overcoming-mental-obstacles-emotional-barriers-downsizing/

Brodsky, S. (2018, November 28). *What Are USDA Loans and How Do They Work?* Credit Karma. https://www.creditkarma.com/home-loans/i/guide-to-usda-loans

Bundrick, H. M. (2020, May 14). *What is a USDA Loan? Am I Eligible for One?* NerdWallet. https://www.nerdwallet.com/article/mortgages/usda-loan

Business, I. (2017, January 16). *How to Earn Passive Income: 22 Ways to Create Multiple Streams of Income*. CityAM. https://www.cityam.com/earn-passive-income-22-ways-create-multiple-streams-income/

Capitol, W. (2018, February 19). *Secured vs. Unsecured Lines of Credit | Fora Financial Blog.* Fora Financial. https://www.forafinancial.com/blog/working-capital/differences-secured-unsecured-lines-credit/

CEPF, L. G. T. (2020, October 20). *A USDA loan is a Mortgage for Homes in Rural or Suburban Counties, and You Don't Need any Money for a Down Payment.* Business Insider. https://www.businessinsider.com/personal-finance/usda-loan?IR=T#the-pros-and-cons-of-a-usda-loan

CEPF, L. G. T. (2021, February 23). *An FHA loan is backed by the government, and it's easier to get than a conventional mortgage.* Business Insider. https://www.businessinsider.com/personal-finance/fha-loan?IR=T#what-is-an-fha-loan

CEPF, T. L., Laura Grace Tarpley. (2021, June 11). *How to Save Money for a House, Whether You're Buying Next Year or 5 Years From Now.* Business Insider. https://www.businessinsider.com/personal-finance/how-to-save-money-for-a-house-automatic?IR=T

Complete List of USDA Loan Benefits and Advantages. (n.d.). USDA Loans. Retrieved July 5, 2021, from https://www.usdaloans.com/program/benefits/

Davis, S. (2013, November 6). *How To Qualify For An FHA Loan.* Money under 30; Money Under 30. https://www.moneyunder30.com/qualify-fha-loan

Dealing With Emotions of Downsizing | Where You Live Matters. (2020, October 15). ASHA.

https://www.whereyoulivematters.org/dealing-with-downsizing-emotions/

Dunn, E. (2020, July 31). *What Is an FHA Loan and How Does It Work?* Credit Karma. https://www.creditkarma.com/home-loans/i/fha-loans

Eisenberg, R. (2014, November 5). *5 Tips for Getting the Best Home Equity Credit Line.* MarketWatch. https://www.marketwatch.com/story/5-tips-for-getting-the-best-home-equity-credit-line-2014-11-05

Eligibility Requirements for USDA Loans - Do you qualify? (n.d.). USDA Loans. Retrieved July 5, 2021, from https://www.usdaloans.com/program/eligibility/

Farrington, R. (2021, March 24). *30 Passive Income Ideas To Build Real Wealth.* The College Investor. https://thecollegeinvestor.com/16399/20-passive-income-ideas/

Fay, B. (2012). *What Is a Personal Line of Credit & How Do They Work?* Debt.org. https://www.debt.org/credit/lines/

FHA Loan - Overview, How to Apply & Qualify for an FHA Loan. (n.d.). Corporate Finance Institute. Retrieved July 5, 2021, from https://corporatefinanceinstitute.com/resources/knowledge/finance/fha-loan/

FHA Loans: Everything You Need to Know | The Truth About Mortgage. (n.d.). Www.thetruthaboutmortgage.com. https://www.thetruthaboutmortgage.com/fha-loans/

Folger, J. (2021, May 23). *The 7 Best Places to Put Your Savings.* Investopedia. https://www.investopedia.com/financial-edge/0810/the-7-best-places-to-put-your-savings.aspx

Fontinelle, A. (2020, June 9). *What is a VA Loan?* Forbes Advisor. https://www.forbes.com/advisor/mortgages/what-is-a-va-loan/

Ford, K. (2020, November 5). *What Are the Basic Types of FHA loans?* FHA Loans. https://www.fhaloans.com/articles/types-of-fha-loans/

Franklin, J. B. (2021, June 21). *10 Ways To Get The Best HELOC Rate.* Bankrate. https://www.bankrate.com/home-equity/get-the-best-heloc-rate/

Frequently Asked Questions. (2018). Usda.gov. https://www.usda.gov/reconnect/frequently-asked-questions

Frequently asked USDA Housing Loan Questions. (2014, December 30). USDA Mortgage Source. https://www.usdamortgagesource.com/blog/frequently-asked-usda-rural-housing-loan-questions/

Fundable. (2019). *What is Crowdfunding? Clear, Simple Answer Here.* Fundable. https://www.fundable.com/learn/resources/guides/crowdfunding/what-is-crowdfunding

Green, C. (n.d.). *How to Build a Business Credit Line.* Small Business - Chron.com. Retrieved July 5, 2021, from https://smallbusiness.chron.com/build-business-credit-line-3696.html

Green, D. (2020, November 5). *USDA Loans | USDA Loan Requirements & Rates for 2021*. Mortgage Rates, Mortgage News and Strategy : The Mortgage Reports. https://themortgagereports.com/14969/usda-loans-home-mortgage

Guru, I. (2017, October 31). *12 Key Moments in the History of Crowdfunding*. Medium. https://medium.com/@ImpactGuru/12-key-moments-in-the-history-of-crowdfunding-so-far-3f614273d95

Harvard Medical School, H. (2018, September 1). *Tips to Cope When it's Time to Downsize*. Harvard Health. https://www.health.harvard.edu/mind-and-mood/tips-to-cope-when-its-time-to-downsize

Hayes, A. (2019). *Line of Credit (LOC) Definition*. Investopedia. https://www.investopedia.com/terms/l/lineofcredit.asp

How to Raise Money in Five Easy Steps. (2018, July 30). GoFundMe. https://www.gofundme.com/c/blog/how-to-raise-money

Hund, L. (2020, September 23). *7 Places To Save Your Extra Money*. Bankrate. https://www.bankrate.com/banking/savings/places-to-save-your-extra-money/

Investopedia, T. (2021, April 15). *Secured vs. Unsecured Lines of Credit: What's the Difference?* Investopedia. https://www.investopedia.com/ask/answers/110614/whats-difference-between-secured-line-credit-and-unsecured-line-credit.asp#:~:text=Key%20Takeaways

Johnson, K. (2016, July 5). *Can you crowdfund your down payment?* MortgageLoan.com. https://www.mortgageloan.com/can-you-crowdfund-your-down-payment#Letters-fees-required

Kagan, J. (2020, August 24). *Automatic Savings Plan.* Investopedia. https://www.investopedia.com/terms/a/automatic_savings_plan.asp

Lake, R. (2018, July 5). *Crowdfunding a Mortgage - SmartAsset.* SmartAsset. https://smartasset.com/mortgage/3-things-to-know-about-crowdfunding-a-mortgage

Lake, R. (2020, October 31). *Conventional vs. FHA Loans: Which Is the Better Way to Buy a Home?* The Balance. https://www.thebalance.com/advantages-and-disadvantages-conventional-vs-fha-loans-4164707

Leonetti, A. (n.d.). *Downsizing Your Home: 10 Pros and 10 Cons to Consider Before Moving.* Transtar Moving | Professional Movers Serving South Jersey & Philadelphia. Retrieved July 5, 2021, from https://www.transtarmoving.com/downsizing-your-home-pros-cons/#:~:text=CON%3A%20You

Light, T. (2020, December 9). *Downsizing Your House: A Complete Guide to Downsizing - Titan Storage.* Titan Storage Solutions. https://www.titanstorage.co.uk/blog/downsizing-your-house-a-complete-guide/

London, R. (n.d.). *The Pros and Cons of Downsizing Your Home.* Royal London. Retrieved July 5, 2021, from https://www.royallondon.com/about-us/members/understanding-your-finances/your-personal-finances/the-pros-and-cons-of-downsizing-your-home/

Marquit, M. (2020, April 20). *How to Downsize Your Lifestyle.* MoneyNing. https://moneyning.com/life-style/how-to-downsize-your-lifestyle/

McGurran, B. (2019, September 3). *How Much Should I Save for a Down Payment?* Www.experian.com. https://www.experian.com/blogs/ask-experian/how-much-should-i-save-for-a-down-payment/

Mei, C. (2016, April 4). *4 Tips To Successfully Downsizing Your Home.* MoneyNing. https://moneyning.com/life-style/4-tips-to-successfully-downsizing-your-home/

Mercadante, K. (2017, January 26). *How to Best Save for a Down Payment On a House.* Money under 30; Money Under 30. https://www.moneyunder30.com/save-downpayment-house

Military.com. (n.d.). *Step-by-Step Guide to the VA Loan Process.* Military.com. Retrieved July 5, 2021, from https://www.military.com/money/va-loans/step-by-step-guide-to-the-va-loan-process.html

Nelson, L. (2014, March 2). *Pros and Cons of FHA Loans: The Good, Bad, and Ugly of FHA.* My Mortgage Insider. https://mymortgageinsider.com/pros-and-cons-fha-loans/

Ponder, C. (2021, February 16). *Should You Crowdfund Your Mortgage Down Payment?* The Balance. https://www.thebalance.com/should-you-crowdfund-your-mortgage-down-payment-4176389

Porter, K. (2018, April 19). *What Is a Line of Credit and How Does It Work?* Credit Karma. https://www.creditkarma.com/advice/i/what-is-line-of-credit#:~:text=A%20line%20of%20credit%20is

Pritchard, J. (2020, August 28). *FHA Home Loan Disadvantages and What You Should Know.* The Balance. https://www.thebalance.com/fha-home-loan-pitfalls-315673

Pritchard, J. (2020, September 20). *How a Line of Credit Works Differently From a Standard Loan.* The Balance. https://www.thebalance.com/how-a-line-of-credit-works-315642

Pritchard, J. (2021, March 1). *What Is an FHA Loan?* The Balance. https://www.thebalance.com/fha-loan-basics-315656

Real Estate Crowdfunding For Your Next House – Real Estate 101 – Trulia Blog. (2015, December 2). Trulia's Blog. https://www.trulia.com/blog/real-estate-crowdfunding/

Riggs, N. (n.d.). *5 Places to Set and Forget Your Money to Let It Grow.* Busy Living Better. https://www.busylivingbetter.com/5-places-to-set-and-forget-your-money-to-let-it-grow/

Rose, J. (2018, July 26). *23 Passive Income Ideas You Can Start Today [Make Money 24/7].* Good Financial Cents®. https://www.goodfinancialcents.com/passive-income-ideas/

Satov, T. (2021, Spring 6). *What Is a Line of Credit and How Does It Work? | Greedyrates.ca.* GreedyRates.

https://www.greedyrates.ca/blog/what-is-a-line-of-credit/

Segal, T. (2019). *Federal Housing Administration Loan – FHA Loan Definition*. Investopedia. https://www.investopedia.com/terms/f/fhaloan.asp

Shin, L. (2015, February 26). *44 Ways To Make More Money*. Forbes. https://www.forbes.com/sites/laurashin/2015/02/26/44-ways-to-make-more-money/?sh=303287917575

Simon, J. (2019, October 29). *What Is a USDA Loan and How to Qualify for One?* SmartAsset. https://smartasset.com/mortgage/what-is-a-usda-loan

Streit, K. (2018, December 15). *The Innovative Down Payment Saving Method You're Not Using*. Apartment Therapy. https://www.apartmenttherapy.com/down-payment-assistance-crowdfunding-homefundit-feather-the-nest-264903

The History of Crowdfunding | Fundable. (2009). Fundable.com. https://www.fundable.com/crowdfunding101/history-of-crowdfunding

Thompson, M. (n.d.). *5 Unexpected Benefits of Downsizing to a Smaller House*. Blog.ditech.com. Retrieved July 5, 2021, from http://blog.ditech.com/blog/5-unexpected-benefits-of-downsizing-to-a-smaller-house

Top 10 Benefits of Downsizing into a Smaller Home. (2013, July 16). MYMOVE. https://www.mymove.com/moving/guides/benefits-of-downsizing-into-a-smaller-home/

Twin, A. (2019). *Open-End Credit: Credit Cards and Loans That Can Be Used Repeatedly*. Investopedia. https://www.investopedia.com/terms/o/openendcredit.asp

USDA Loans: Meaning, Process & Requirements. (2021, May 21). Www.rocketmortgage.com. https://www.rocketmortgage.com/learn/usda-loans

VA Loan Eligibility Requirements. (n.d.). Veterans United Home Loans. https://www.veteransunited.com/va-loans/va-home-loan-eligibility/

VA Loans: The Complete Guide by Veterans United Home Loans. (n.d.). Veterans United Home Loans. Retrieved July 5, 2021, from https://www.veteransunited.com/va-loans/

Veterans Affairs, U. S. D. of. (2020, October 1). *Eligibility Requirements for VA Home Loan Programs*. Veterans Affairs. https://www.va.gov/housing-assistance/home-loans/eligibility/

Veterans Affairs, U. S. Dept. of. (2016, October 12). *Ten Things Most Veterans Don't Know about VA home loans*. VAntage Point. https://blogs.va.gov/VAntage/31825/ten-things-veterans-dont-know-va-home-loans/

Veterans Affairs, U. S. Dept. of. (2020, April 30). *How to Apply for a VA Home Loan Certificate of Eligibility*. Veterans Affairs. https://www.va.gov/housing-assistance/home-loans/how-to-apply/

Vohwinkle, J. (2020, August 29). *Why You Need an Automatic Savings Plan*. The Balance. https://www.thebalance.com/how-to-create-an-automatic-savings-plan-1289900

Warren, K. (2021, February 16). *USDA Home Loans: What They Are and How They Work*. MoneyGeek.com. https://www.moneygeek.com/mortgage/usda-loans/

What Is A USDA Loan? Rates And Eligibility. (2021, April 5). Www.quickenloans.com. https://www.quickenloans.com/learn/benefits-usda-loans

What to Know If You Downsize Your Home to Save Money | Discover. (2017, November 27). Discover Bank - Banking Topics Blog. https://www.discover.com/online-banking/banking-topics/downsize-your-home-to-save-money/

Wichter, Z. (2021, January 4). *What Is An FHA Loan? | 2020 Complete Guide*. Bankrate. https://www.bankrate.com/mortgages/what-is-an-fha-loan/

Wichter, Z. (2021, January 5). *VA Loans: Everything Veterans And Service Members Need To Know*. Bankrate. https://www.bankrate.com/mortgages/understanding-va-loans/

Wood, K. (2021, February 22). *FHA Loan: What to Know | 2021 Guidelines*. NerdWallet. https://www.nerdwallet.com/article/mortgages/fha-loan

www.ingramcontent.com/pod-product-compliance
Lightning Source LLC
Chambersburg PA
CBHW031428210526
45464CB00005B/2096